Writing Engagement
Involving Students in the Writing Process:
Grade 6

By
JANET P. SITTER, Ph.D.

COPYRIGHT © Mark Twain Media, Inc.

ISBN 1-58037-199-X

Printing No. CD-1545

Mark Twain Media, Inc., Publishers
Distributed by Carson-Dellosa Publishing Company, Inc.

Table of Contents

Table of Contents

Introduction

This book is a writing engagement resource for both teachers and students. Through these exercises students will improve both their writing and their language skills. By evaluating their writing using the rubrics provided, students will sharpen both their understanding of the writing process and their writing skills. Teachers will also have a consistent process for teaching and evaluating student writing using the rubrics.

Five features highlight this book: (1) the practice and apply student work pages, (2) the teacher evaluation rubrics, (3) the student writing rubrics, (4) the student test writing prompts, and (5) the writing skills tests.

The Writing Process

1. **Prewriting** – Choose a topic; gather and organize ideas; identify the audience for the writing; identify the purpose of the writing; choose the appropriate format for the writing.

2. **Drafting** – Write a rough draft to get down the ideas; write beginnings that "grab" the reader's attention; emphasize ideas rather than mechanics.

3. **Revising** – Share writing with a group or teacher; reflect on comments and make substantive changes; prepare a clean draft.

4. **Editing** – Proofread narratives carefully; help others proofread; identify and correct mechanical errors.

5. **Publishing** – Publish writing in an appropriate form; share writing with an appropriate audience.

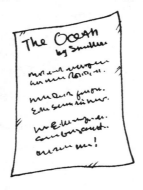

Section I: Writing for a Purpose and an Audience

Purpose: Am I writing to entertain? To inform? To persuade? To describe?

Audience: Am I writing for myself, to express and clarify my ideas and/or feelings? Or am I writing for others? Possible audiences include other children, younger children, parents, grandparents, children's authors, pen pals, etc.

Unit 1: Writing To Express Ideas

Purpose: Writing to learn and explore ideas and problems

Audience: Usually done for general, unknown audiences

Unit 2: Writing To Inform

Purpose: Writing to share information with others

Audience: The audience may be known or unknown.

Unit 3: Writing To Influence

Purpose: Writing to sway opinions and convince someone to accept the writer's way of thinking

Audience: The audience may be known or unknown.

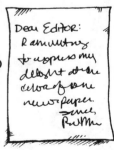

Unit 4: Writing To Entertain or Create

Purpose: To create fictitious stories, true stories, poetry, or plays to entertain others

Audience: Classmates, family, other trusted audiences

Unit 1: Writing to Express Ideas—Narrative Writing

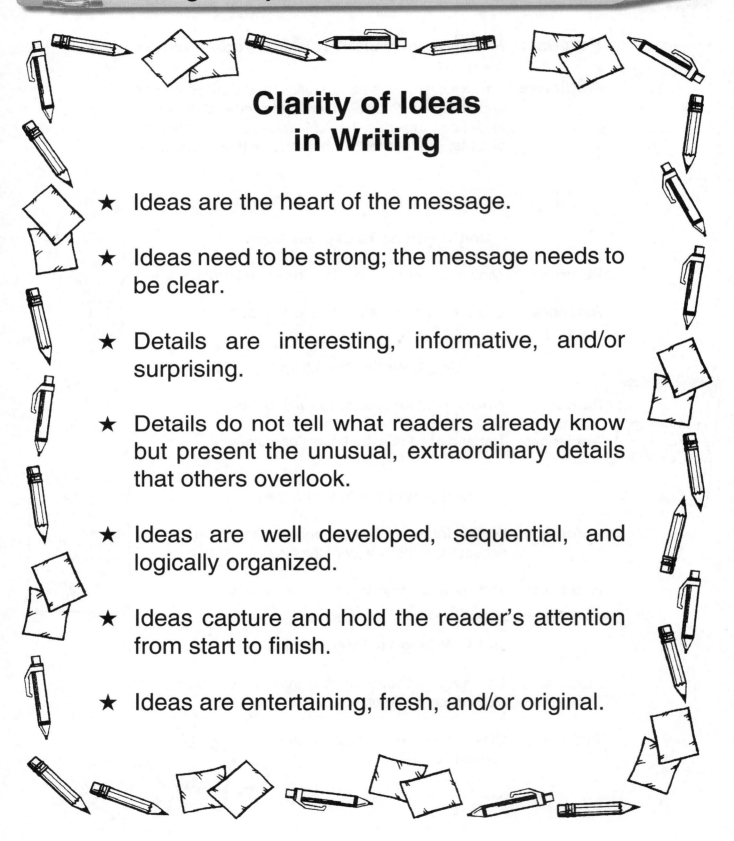

Clarity of Ideas in Writing

★ Ideas are the heart of the message.

★ Ideas need to be strong; the message needs to be clear.

★ Details are interesting, informative, and/or surprising.

★ Details do not tell what readers already know but present the unusual, extraordinary details that others overlook.

★ Ideas are well developed, sequential, and logically organized.

★ Ideas capture and hold the reader's attention from start to finish.

★ Ideas are entertaining, fresh, and/or original.

Name: _____   Date: _____

Unit 1: Teacher Evaluation Writing Rubric—Ideas

Topic: _____

Type of Writing: *Expository*   *Persuasive*   *Narrative*

Directions: Circle the number that best describes the quality of the writing.

Criteria for Writing Rubric: Ideas

Features	Not yet	Emerging	Developing	Competent	Strong
Ideas/Content:	1	2	3	4	5
	Writer is unclear about topic and/or purpose. Details are confusing, overwhelming, or missing. Reads like a series of random, unconnected thoughts. Unable to separate main points from details. Reader must do more work than the writer to understand.	Writer has purpose, though it may be unclear to reader. Main idea and details are indistinguishable from one another. Needs major work on topic development and using details. No understanding of topic sentences. Reader would have difficulty stating main idea but could tell you the topic of the paper.	Writer has vague sense of purpose but not audience. Ideas and information are reasonably clear, though important information may be missing. Details, if present, are sketchy or not well integrated with main idea. Beginning use of topic sentences, but sometimes has trouble staying on topic.	Writer is clear about purpose and audience. Paper is focused and holds reader's attention. Details add to the whole and are necessary to the paper. Paper has clear sense of topic development. Topic itself is important/ informative. More attention to quality of details than quantity of details.	Writer clearly and thoughtfully expresses ideas in a new, interesting way. Details and examples are carefully chosen to enhance main idea. Paper is focused, purposeful, and captures the reader's attention. Reader feels satisfied, better for having read the paper.

Comments: _____

_____

Name: _____   Date: _____

Unit 1: Student Writing Rubric—Ideas

Topic: _____

Type of Writing: *Expository*   *Persuasive*   *Narrative*

Directions: Check those statements that apply to your piece of writing.

_____   I have a clear and interesting topic.

_____   My writing is based on my own experience or my own investigation of the topic.

_____   I can sum up my main point in one sentence:

_____

_____

_____   My beginning "grabs" my readers' attention and makes them want to read more.

_____   All my sentences are important to the topic.

_____   I included all important events in the order of their happening.

_____   I *show* things happening rather than *telling* about them.

_____   I have a strong ending that leaves my readers satisfied.

_____   My readers aren't left with any important unanswered questions.

Comments: _____

_____

_____

_____

_____

_____

_____

_____

_____

Unit 1: Writing a Personal Narrative—A Memoir

Key Ideas

- **A personal narrative** is a true story about something that happened to the person who tells it.

- **A memoir** is a true story, a personal narrative, that is built on the memory of the writer.

- **Memoirs** have the following characteristics:
    - They are told in the first person, "I."
    - They are very descriptive accounts, so the reader can experience what the writer experienced.
    - They have well-developed, believable characters.
    - They create details that support the topic even if they aren't "true" to the original memory.
    - They use realistic dialogue to help support the memory and the characters.

Practice

Directions: Read the personal narrative below and answer the questions that follow.

The Lions Carnival
by Nettie

Going back to school was always exciting for me and my friends because following that big day was "The Lions Carnival," my favorite event of the small town in which we lived. The carnival brought the noise of the old-time fire engine, the siren of the purple locomotive, and the yelling of the barker for the cake walk. This little carnival was big! Twenty or thirty red wagons tied together full of hundreds of squealing, laughing, shouting children (and a few over-protective mothers or fathers scrunched up in the small wagons) were pulled around and around the square. When you were too big for the wagons and the five-foot ferris wheel, you moved on to the fire engine or the purple locomotive. Finally, as a teenager, you got to ride the bucking bronco ... a telephone pole rigged out with a dozen horse saddles, pulled by a car missing its shocks. What fun! It was around this age you were allowed to go "uptown," without your parents, to hang out at the carnival. What freedom! The fall air, the blare of the siren, the noise of the crowd, the smell of the fried fish ... Wow, it must be fall in Carlinville!

---

1. How did the writer grab the reader's attention right at the beginning?

   _____

   _____

   _____

   _____

Unit 1: Writing a Personal Narrative—A Memoir (cont.)

2. How did the writer use details to show what she saw, heard, or felt?

_____

_____

_____

_____

3. Is this story told in the author's voice? What clues do you have to support this?

_____

_____

_____

_____

4. Does the narrative have an interesting ending that tells how the story worked out for the author or how the author felt? What is it?

_____

_____

_____

_____

5. Is this a personal narrative? Why? _____

_____

_____

_____

On Your Own: Think of an event in your life that is truly memorable. It might be a very special memory for you: a place, a happening, a person. Using the characteristics of a memoir, write a brief memoir of the memory. Remember, you can embellish your memory with "fictional events"—just the basic outline of your memoir must be true.

Do you like it? Do others? Keep polishing it until you have a memoir worth publishing.

Name: _____ Date: _____

Unit 1: Writing a Myth

Key Idea

- A **myth** is a story made up to explain how the world works. Many years ago, people used **myths** to explain how the world operated. They believed that the forces of nature and their own actions were controlled by various gods, people, and animals with supernatural powers.

Practice

1. Read the myth below that tells how Saint Nicholas became the patron saint of children.

    A citizen of Patara had lost all his money and had to support three young daughters who could not find husbands because they were so poor. They had no money for a dowry, and the man couldn't support them any longer, so he was going to give them over to the poor house. Nicholas, the bishop of Myra in the fourth century, heard of this problem and under darkness threw a bag of gold in the open window of the man's house. This was the dowry for the oldest girl, and she was soon married and spared life as a slave in the poor house. At intervals, Nicholas did the same for the second and third daughters, and they too were married. The last time, the father was on the watch. He recognized his benefactor and overwhelmed him with his gratitude.

    From then on, St. Nicholas became known as the special protector of children.

2. Invent a myth of your own. Your myth could explain one of the following topics or another of your own choice. First draft a short outline of your myth.

Why the grass is green	Why the sky is blue
Why earthquakes happen	Why the wind blows
Why some trees are always green	Why people grow old
Why the rain falls	Why dogs are friendly to humans

3. Once you are satisfied with your basic idea, write a first draft of the myth on another sheet of paper. Be sure to keep cause and effect very clear, and check your evaluation sheet on clarity of writing.

4. Revise, edit, polish, and publish your myth in a big book with those of your classmates.

Name: _____ Date: _____

Unit 1: Writing E-mail

Key Ideas

- Electronic mail (**e-mail**) is different from writing a letter or talking on the phone.

- **E-mail** messages are typically more direct and shorter than regular letters.

- General rules for **e-mail** are:
    1. Give your message a specific title in the subject line. The receiver should know the subject before opening the e-mail.
    2. Keep your paragraphs and sentences short. It is difficult to read long paragraphs and sentences on the screen.
    3. Skip a line *instead of indenting* when you begin a new paragraph. Your message will be easier for the receiver to read on the screen.
    4. Remember that special type like *italics* and/or **bold** may not show up on your receiver's screen.

    5. Use humor carefully. Your receiver cannot see your face, hear your voice tone, or understand your sarcasm. He or she may not know that you are joking.
    6. Follow the rules of good writing. An e-mail is more casual than a letter, but what you say and how you say it reflects on *you*.
    7. Proofread your messages, and fix all capitalization, punctuation, usage, and spelling mistakes before sending your e-mail.
    8. Be sure that e-mail is the *best* way to send your message. Sometimes the phone or a letter is better.

Practice

1. Read this e-mail from Nick. Using the criteria listed above, critique his e-mail. How could he rewrite his e-mail to make it meet the criteria?

From: Nick
To: Bro'
Date: April 11
Subject:
Hey bro I'm just writing to make sure you're ok and not still mad at me about the accident this mornin. But I still think its partly your fault if you hadn't been riding so fast I would have been able to stop sooner. I flew over my handle bars too ya know. Any way Cheer up gravel cuts never leave scars. Well I gotta run. Later.

Name: _____ Date: _____

Unit 1: Writing E-mail (cont.)

2. Rewrite Nick's e-mail here so that it meets all the criteria.

    _____

    _____

    _____

    _____

    _____

    _____

    _____

    _____

    _____

    _____

3. Now, you try it. Draft an e-mail message to a friend of yours in which you tell him or her some important news.

    From: _____

    To: _____

    Date: _____

    Subject: _____

    _____

    _____

    _____

    _____

    _____

    _____

    _____

    _____

On Your Own: Be sure you've checked punctuation, capitalization, spelling, and usage.

Name: _____ Date: _____

Unit 1: Writing a Book Review

Key Ideas

- Even when a group of students reads the same book, students may choose a different part or character of the book to report on.

- Individual tastes and different experiences and backgrounds help determine the answers to the opinions below.

Practice

1. Read a book and choose one to write an opinion about. Don't worry if others have read the same book.

2. Write your opinion about the book on the lines below.

   a. Title of the book: _____

   b. Author/Illustrator: _____

   c. My favorite part of the book was: _____

   _____

   _____

   _____

   (pages): _____ (paragraphs): _____

   d. I liked the story when the character(s) did or said: _____

   _____

   _____

   _____

   (pages): _____ (paragraphs): _____

   e. I felt (circle one)   happy   sad   scared   excited

                                   surprised   bored   nervous   joyful

   when: _____

   _____

   _____

   _____

   (pages): _____ (paragraphs): _____

Unit 1: Writing a Book Review (cont.)

f. The story's (circle one)   plot   character(s)   setting

reminded me of: _____

_____

_____

_____

_____

_____

(pages): _____ (paragraphs): _____

g. A "quotable quote" from the book that made me think in a new way or moved me in some way was:

_____

_____

_____

_____

_____

_____

(pages): _____ (paragraphs): _____

h. This quote was said by: _____

(pages) _____ and is important in the story because:

_____

_____

_____

_____

_____

On Your Own: Now take all this brainstorming work that you've done and write your opinion essay in narrative form. Remember the rules of writing, and remember especially to make your writing clear.

Name: _____ Date: _____

Unit 1: Writing Skills Test

Directions: Darken the circle next to the choice that is the <u>best</u> answer.

1. When writing to express ideas, it is most important to know which one of these?
   - ○ A. Who your audience is
   - ○ B. What your supporting sentences are
   - ○ C. What your closing is going to be
   - ○ D. How old you are

2. When writing to express ideas, it is also important to know which one of these?
   - ○ A. How to write paragraphs
   - ○ B. How to write a complete sentence
   - ○ C. What your purpose is
   - ○ D. What your title is going to be

3. Finally, when writing to express ideas, it is also important to know which one of these?
   - ○ A. The writing format you need
   - ○ B. What you want to say
   - ○ C. What you enjoy about writing
   - ○ D. How long it will take you to write

4. Which of these (there may be more than one) describes the differences between e-mail and a letter?
   - ○ A. A true story that happened to the author
   - ○ B. A more direct and shorter communication
   - ○ C. Follows the rules of good writing carefully
   - ○ D. Contains a subject line

5. Which of these <u>best</u> describes a myth?
   - ○ A. A true story that happened to the author
   - ○ B. A story that reports the feelings of the author
   - ○ C. A letter written to request, inform, or complain, usually to someone the writer doesn't know
   - ○ D. A story made up to explain how the world works

6. Which of these <u>best</u> describes a personal narrative?
   - ○ A. A true story that happened to the author
   - ○ B. A story that reports the feelings of the author
   - ○ C. A letter written to request, inform, or complain, usually to someone the writer doesn't know
   - ○ D. A letter written to a person the writer knows well

Name: _____ Date: _____

Unit 1: Writing Skills Test (cont.)

7. Which of these best describes a memoir?
   ○ A. A true story that happened to the author
   ○ B. A story that reports the feelings of the author
   ○ C. A story built around the memory of the author; not all parts may be true
   ○ D. A letter written to a person the writer knows well

8. All but one of these describes the characteristics of a memoir. Which does not?
   ○ A. They are told in the first person "I."
   ○ B. They are very descriptive accounts so the reader can experience what the writer experienced.
   ○ C. They have well-developed, believable characters.
   ○ D. They use rhythm and rhyme to tell the story.

9. Which one of these is true for writing an opinion essay?
   ○ A. Individual tastes and different experiences and backgrounds help determine people's opinions of books and movies.
   ○ B. It is important to state your opinion clearly and succinctly.
   ○ C. You must include a "quotable quote" in your opinion essay.
   ○ D. It is helpful to figure out a solution to a problem you have.

10. Which one of these is true for writing to express an idea?
    ○ A. It is usually done for general, unknown audiences.
    ○ B. It is important for the ideas to be strong and the message to be clear.
    ○ C. Ideas are what capture and hold the reader's attention from start to finish.
    ○ D. All of these are important when writing to express an idea.

Name: _____ Date: _____

Unit 1: Writing Skills Test (cont.)

11. Writing Sample: **Prejudice: The Activist**

• Write a public service campaign. Create advertisements and public service announcements on television and radio educating the community about prejudice.

• Before you begin writing, use scratch paper to organize your ideas.

• Use the best English you can, but do not worry about mistakes. It is most important to be clear so that the person reading your writing is aware of your views and opinions on prejudice. Your writing will be evaluated especially for clarity of ideas.

_____

_____

_____

_____

_____

_____

_____

_____

_____

_____

_____

_____

_____

_____

Unit 2: Writing to Inform—Expository Writing

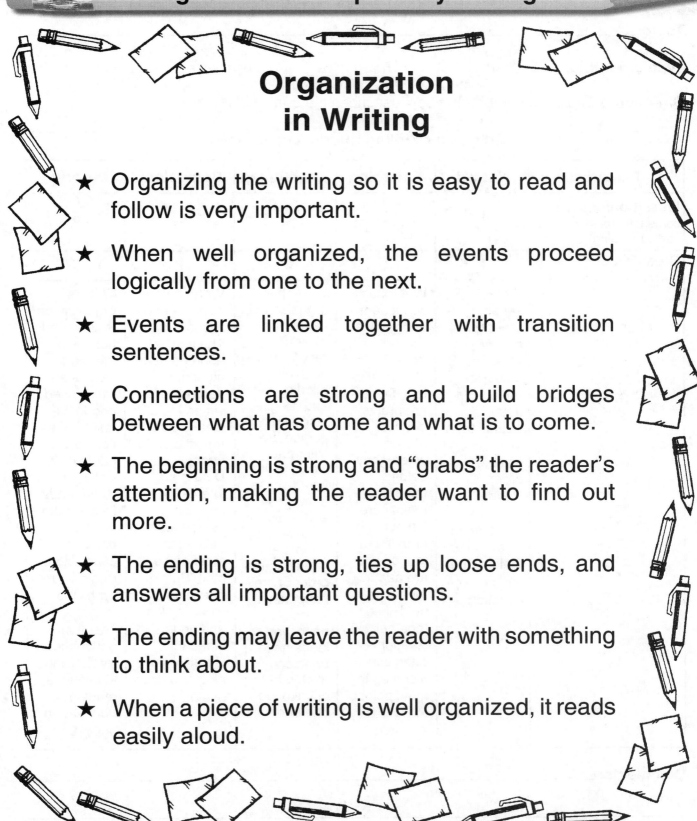

Organization in Writing

★ Organizing the writing so it is easy to read and follow is very important.

★ When well organized, the events proceed logically from one to the next.

★ Events are linked together with transition sentences.

★ Connections are strong and build bridges between what has come and what is to come.

★ The beginning is strong and "grabs" the reader's attention, making the reader want to find out more.

★ The ending is strong, ties up loose ends, and answers all important questions.

★ The ending may leave the reader with something to think about.

★ When a piece of writing is well organized, it reads easily aloud.

Name: _____ Date: _____

Unit 2: Teacher Evaluation Writing Rubric—Organization

Topic: _____

Type of Writing: *Expository*   *Persuasive*   *Narrative*

Directions: Circle the number that best describes the quality of the writing.

Criteria for Writing Rubric: Organization

Features	Not yet	Emerging	Developing	Competent	Strong
Ideas/Content: Is the content focused, original, and interesting?	1	2	3	4	5
Organization:	1	2	3	4	5
	Writer lacks sense of organization. Main ideas can't be separated from details. Events told in no recognizable order. Reader is confused about main idea and/or topic. Paper has no direction.	Writer has some sense of organization but doesn't always stick to it. Details are present but not always where they belong. Important events are left out and/or unimportant ones are added. Ideas are not linked together. Reader is often confused as to main point of the writing.	Writer has organization; paper has clear and recognizable beginning, middle, and end. Beginning and ending are still rather weak. Writer has a sense of purpose and is aware of audience. Events are related in the order of their happening. Transitions need work; ideas need to be connected and/or linked to one another.	Writer has clear organizational plan. The plan is appropriate to audience and purpose of writer. Main idea is clear, transitions are strong. Details are interesting and connected to main idea most of the time. Sequencing of ideas is clear and understandable. Good beginning and good ending.	Writer's organization is clear and helpful to the reader. Details are well placed and fit the text. Transitions are particularly well done; writer leads reader from point, to point, to conclusion. Beginning *grabs* the reader's attention and makes reader want to continue reading. Very strong ending.

Comments: _____

_____

Unit 2: Student Writing Rubric—Organization

Topic: _____

Type of Writing: *Expository*   *Persuasive*   *Narrative*

Directions: Check those statements that apply to your writing.

_____ I have a clear and interesting topic.

_____ My beginning "grabs" my readers' attention and makes them want to read more.

_____ My writing is easy to follow. Each point leads to the next point.

_____ I include all important events in the order of their happening.

_____ My details add to the story and make it more colorful and interesting.

_____ I *show* things happening rather than *telling* about them.

_____ I include dialogue when appropriate.

_____ I have a strong ending that leaves my readers satisfied.

_____ My ending tells how the story worked out or how I felt about it.

_____ There aren't any important unanswered questions in my story.

Comments: _____

_____

_____

_____

_____

_____

_____

Name: _____ Date: _____

Unit 2: Writing to Compare and Contrast

Key Ideas

- When we look at the similarities of two alternatives, we **compare**.

- When we look at the differences of two alternatives, we **contrast**.

- The word **comparison** is often used to include both comparison and contrast.

- **Compare/contrast essays** explain similarities and differences between two objects, actions, ideas, concepts, or situations. **A compare/contrast essay** may also present the advantages and disadvantages of one of the elements.

- Writing that **compares and contrasts** leads to more thoughtful decision-making.

Practice

Directions: Write a compare/contrast essay about one of the topics listed below. Compare the objects (e.g., tell how they are similar), and then contrast the objects (tell how they are different). Finally, present the advantages and disadvantages of one over the other.

dog - cat	sand - clay	Mac - PC
desk - chair	cracker - cookie	boots - shoes
spoon - fork	glove - mitten	brush - comb
CD - tape	VCR - DVD	milk - water

1. On the lines below, write a great introduction that immediately grabs your reader's interest.

   _____

   _____

   _____

   _____

   _____

   _____

   _____

2. Continue on your own paper. Write the middle of the essay, including the parts described in the directions.

3. Finally, write a great conclusion, one that finishes the essay and brings a sense of satisfaction and closure for the reader.

Name: _____ Date: _____

Unit 2: Writing About Advantages and Disadvantages

Key Ideas
- When we look at the similarities of two alternatives, we **compare**.

- When we look at the differences of two alternatives, we **contrast**.

- The word **comparison** is often used to include both comparison and contrast.

- **Compare/contrast essays** explain similarities and differences between two objects, actions, ideas, concepts, or situations. **A compare/contrast essay** may also present the advantages and disadvantages of one of the elements.

- Writing that **compares and contrasts** leads to more thoughtful decision-making.

Practice

Directions: Compare/contrast essays can take the form of determining the advantages and disadvantages of everyday activities such as those in the list below. Choose one and write a compare/contrast essay about it that emphasizes the advantages and disadvantages.

> Being required to participate in physical education
> Shortening the school day
> Having more homework
> Watching less television
> Being the oldest (or youngest, middle, or only) child in the family

1. In the space below, write a great introduction that immediately grabs your reader's interest.

_____

_____

_____

_____

_____

_____

_____

_____

2. Continue on your own paper. Write the middle of the essay, which describes the advantages and disadvantages of the issue.

3. Finally, write a great conclusion, one that finishes the essay and brings a sense of satisfaction and closure for the reader.

Name: _____ Date: _____

Unit 2: Writing a How-To Essay

Key Ideas
- A **how-to essay** explains in detail how to do something, but it also serves as a piece of communication from one person to other people.

- Some common characteristics of a **how-to essay** include:
  - An introduction that "grabs" the reader's interest;
  - Steps of the process in sequence and in logical order;
  - A full explanation including details and examples of each step in the process;
  - Reasons for the steps including negative directions;
  - Illustrations that may accompany the text; and
  - A conclusion that summarizes an outcome.

Practice

Directions: Follow the steps below to develop your how-to essay.

1. **Topic Selection:** Think of a topic of interest from a recent social studies or science unit of study or use one of the suggestions below.

   > How is hail formed?
   > How does our body make blood?
   > How is a mountain range formed?
   > How does a television work?
   > How do birds migrate?

2. Once you have your topic selected (Be sure to select one you know something about or can research some information about.), do some brainstorming of the steps involved in the process. Use the space below for notes.

_____

_____

_____

_____

_____

_____

_____

_____

Name: _____ Date: _____

Unit 2: Writing a How-To Essay (cont.)

3. **Introduction:** The first thing you want to do in the introduction is to "grab" your reader's attention. There are a number of interesting ways to do this.

    -   *Ask a question:* Do you enjoy chewing gum? Do you know how it is made?
    -   *Tell a vignette (a brief story about the topic):* I remember so clearly the day my mom tried to get the chewing gum out of my hair. "How is this stuff made?" she cried in frustration. Now I know the answer.
    -   *Explain the importance of the subject:* Why chew gum? It's not really food. You're not supposed to swallow it. It loses its flavor. It sticks to people's shoes. Because it's fun. It's something to do, and some say it even increases concentration, relieves boredom, and relaxes a person.
    -   *Present a startling fact:* Both the ancient Greeks and the Mayan Indians enjoyed chewing gum, but it wasn't until the 1860s that modern chewing gum was manufactured.

    Work on your interest grabber:

    _____

    _____

    _____

    _____

    _____

    _____

    An introduction for a how-to essay may also include a description of the basic materials, equipment, and supplies needed to complete the task. This is especially important if you plan to demonstrate how to do something. List your materials and equipment here:

    _____

    _____

    _____

    _____

4. Now you are ready to draft your essay. Remember to use transitional words to help organize and put your essay in chronological order (e.g., *first, second, third; next, then, before, after, finally, last, in conclusion*).

    Draft your essay on your own paper. Don't forget to use your "grabber" opening. Review the characteristics listed at the beginning of this lesson. Your conclusion is as important as your opening, so spend some quality time thinking on it.

Unit 2: Writing About Cause and Effect

Key Ideas
- **A cause** is something that makes something else happen; an **effect** is the thing that happens.

- When you write **cause-and-effect essays**, you usually know what the effect is, and you are trying to discover what caused it.
  - *Examples:*   *Why do CDs cost more than tapes?*
    Why are all the fish in the lake dying?

- Some characteristics of **cause-and-effect** writing are:
  - Introductions usually establish the situation or question to be explained or problem to be solved.

  - Writers use transitional words for cause and effect in the body of their essays: *because, as a result, thus, consequently, therefore, since, so that, in order that, in order to, as if, hence.*

  - Writers focus on primary causes and primary effects in their writing.

  - Conclusions emphasize a specific result, a long-term effect, a solution to a problem, or a summary of the importance of the explanation.

Practice

Directions: Choose one of the topics listed below to write a cause and effect essay about or choose one of your own that has been approved by your teacher.

> Why is the sky blue?
> What are the effects of hurricanes or tornadoes?
> Why are we being plagued by mosquitoes on the playground?
> Why are butterfly wings so colorful?
> Why does the earth have only one moon?

1. Write a great introduction that immediately grabs your reader's interest.

_____

_____

_____

_____

_____

_____

_____

Name: _____ Date: _____

Unit 2: Writing About Cause and Effect (cont.)

2. Explore the causes and effects of your question using the following heuristic:

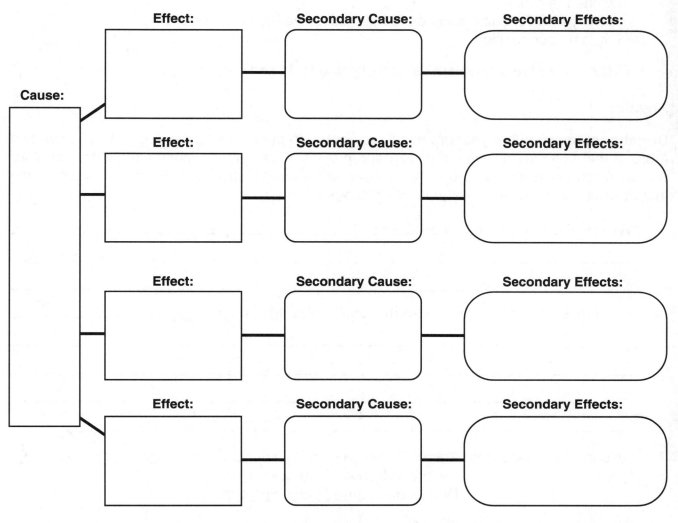

3. Finally, write a great conclusion, one that finishes the essay and brings a sense of satisfaction and closure for the reader.

_____

_____

_____

_____

_____

_____

Name: _____ Date: _____

Unit 2: Writing to Solve a Problem

Key Ideas

- When **writing to solve a problem**, you:
  - Define the problem;
  - Identify and consult resources to help you solve the problem; and
  - Explain your solution.

- **Writing to solve a problem** requires finding facts and information.

Practice

Directions: Imagine that your parents have agreed to get a new family dog … IF you can find a breed that everyone in the family can agree upon. One person wants a small dog, another wants one that is friendly to people but will also serve as a guard dog. Your mother wants a dog that doesn't shed, and your sister is allergic to pet dander.

1. What is the problem you need to solve? _____

   _____

   _____

2. What resources can provide information to solve this problem? _____

   _____

   _____

   _____

   _____

   Also try these websites: Animal Planet's Guide to Your Dog, http://animal.discover.com
   American Kennel Club, www.aka.org
   Dog Domain, http://petstation.com

Name: _____ Date: _____

Unit 2: Writing to Solve a Problem (cont.)

3. Take notes on information that will help you solve this problem: _____

    _____

    _____

    _____

    _____

    _____

    _____

    _____

4. Write a summary that restates the problem and explains the actions taken to solve the problem.

    _____

    _____

    _____

    _____

    _____

    _____

    _____

5. Describe the solution to the problem and why this is the "perfect" solution to the problem.

    _____

    _____

    _____

    _____

    _____

    _____

    _____

On Your Own: On your own paper, put this information together into an expository essay.

Name: _____ Date: _____

Unit 2: Writing to Fill Out a Form

Key Ideas

- **Forms** are sometimes used to gather information. Different **forms** require different information.

- *Always* check with a parent, guardian, or teacher before providing any information on a **form**.

- It is most important to proofread the **form** to make sure the information you give is correct.

Practice

Guidelines

1. Read all the directions carefully. Look over the entire form first. Ask about any parts you do not understand.

2. Complete the form neatly and legibly. Be sure to print if it says to print. Ask someone to help you with any information you do not know.

3. Sign and date the form.

4. Proofread the form for mistakes. This is very important. Make sure the information you have given is correct and that you have completed all areas on the form.

5. Return or mail your completed form to the place from which you received it.

Directions: On the following page is a School Information Form. Practice filling out the form correctly and neatly. You may have to ask family members for certain information.

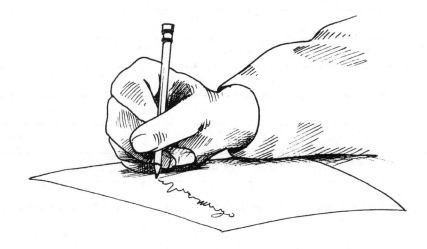

Name: _____   Date: _____

Unit 2: Writing to Fill Out a Form (cont.)

SCHOOL INFORMATION FORM

Grade _____

Last Name _____

First Name _____   Middle Initial _____

Street Address _____

City, State, Zip _____

Phone # _____   Sex: M   F   Race _____

Birthdate _____   Soc. Sec. # _____

Mother: Work Phone # _____

Mother: Place of Employment _____

Father: Work Phone # _____

Father: Place of Employment _____

Emergency Contact Person _____

Emergency Phone # _____   Relationship _____

Parent/Guardian _____

Address _____

City, State, Zip _____

Phone _____

Doctor _____   Doctor Phone _____

Dentist _____   Dentist Phone _____

Special Health Concerns _____

_____

_____

Name: _____ Date: _____

Unit 2: Writing an Outline

Key Ideas

- An **outline** is a general plan for your writing. It has a title, main topics, subtopics, and details.

- An **outline** uses a sequence to help you organize ideas for a report or essay.
  - **Chronological order** tells the order in which events happened.
  - **Spacial order** describes the location of things in a place.
  - **Logical order** groups together related ideas, such as details, in order of importance.

Practice

1. A biography would best be arranged in chronological order. Read the following events in the life of Britney Spears. Use time sequence to rearrange the main headings and subheadings in the correct order for the outline.

Education
Parents are Jamie and Lynne Spears
Enjoys romance novels
Sophomore in high school
Member of the Mickey Mouse Club
Sister, Jamie Lynn, 8
Born in Kentwood, Louisiana
Family

Born December 2, 1981
Justin Timberlake
Collects dolls
Travels with a tutor
Brother, Bryan, 21
Childhood
Solo performing
Favorites

I. _____   II. _____

   A. _____   A. _____

   B. _____   B. _____

   C. _____   C. _____

III. _____   IV. _____

   A. _____   A. _____

   B. _____   B. _____

                                            C. _____

                                          D. _____

Name: _____ Date: _____

Unit 2: Writing an Outline (cont.)

2. Suppose you are writing a report about the country of Liechtenstein. You want to describe briefly these four areas: Geography, People, Government, and Major Cities. Using the information provided, fill in the outline below.

Malbun
Central Europe
Population 32,207
German, Alemannic dialect
People
Ethnic groups: Turkish, Italian
Catholic and Protestant
Schaan
Balzers

Government
Principality of Liechtenstein
Capital city: Vaduz
Located between Austria and Switzerland
Voting age: 20 years of age
Hereditary constitutional monarchy
Ruggell
Cold, snowy climate

I. _____

   A. _____

   B. _____

   C. _____

II. _____

   A. _____

   B. _____

   C. _____

   D. _____

III. _____

   A. _____

   B. _____

   C. _____

   D. _____

IV. _____

   A. _____

   B. _____

   C. _____

   D. _____

On Your Own: Now you try it. Choose a topic of special interest to you. Gather information. Figure out your categories, and then outline your information. Write your essay from your outline.

Name: _____ Date: _____

Unit 2: Writing a Research Report

Key Ideas

- **A research report** presents information learned through research about the topic.

- **A good research report** has the following characteristics:
  - Interesting information organized logically;
  - Interest-catching introductory paragraph that tells the main idea;
  - Well-organized paragraphs with topic sentences for each new main idea;
  - Good transitional sentences that lead from one main idea to the next;
  - Written in the writer's own words, not copied from sources;
  - Strong summary/conclusion paragraph that sums up the research; and
  - An accurate listing of all sources.

- **A good research report** begins with an interesting question.

Practice

Directions: Research a famous person who you admire. Write about his/her important accomplishments and struggles and the person's influence on others. Follow the steps below to help organize your writing.

1. **Start Thinking:** Who do you admire? Who do you want to learn more about? List some possible people to research here:

   _____

   _____

   _____

   _____

2. What are some of the things you would like to know about these people?

   _____

   _____

   _____

   _____

   _____

3. Discuss your ideas with a writing partner and/or your teacher. Decide on the best one.

   _____

Name: _____ Date: _____

Unit 2: Writing a Research Report (cont.)

4. Make a K-W-L chart to help you find out about your topic. This can help you determine your outline headings too.

K	W	L
What I Know	*What I Want to Know*	*What I've learned*

5. Now locate information about your topic. Use the Internet and other reference sources. Talk to people; there may be a relative or a local expert on this person.

6. Research your topic and take notes.

_____

_____

_____

_____

_____

_____

_____

_____

_____

_____

_____

7. Turn your notes into an outline.

8. Turn each main heading from your outline into a topic sentence.

9. Write paragraphs from the subheadings and details from your outline.

10. Write an interesting beginning and a strong conclusion for your report.

11. Revise and edit your report. Add graphics and visuals to make it more attractive.

12. Publish your report.

Name: _____ Date: _____

Unit 2: Writing Skills Test

Directions: Darken the circle next to the choice that is the <u>best</u> answer.

1. When writing for organization, which one of these is <u>most</u> important?
   - ○ A. A clear and interesting topic
   - ○ B. Interesting dialogue
   - ○ C. Giving my opinion
   - ○ D. Adding good description

2. When a piece of writing is well organized,
   - ○ A. it has a strong beginning.
   - ○ B. it has a strong ending.
   - ○ C. it reads well aloud.
   - ○ D. all of the above

3. When concentrating on the organization of writing, it is important for the writer to
   - ○ A. provide visual illustrations.
   - ○ B. describe where the supplies are.
   - ○ C. include all events in the order of their happening.
   - ○ D. leave unanswered questions to pique the reader's curiosity.

4. Good organization means
   - ○ A. that the paper is clear and interesting.
   - ○ B. the mechanical correctness of the writing is good.
   - ○ C. that the ideas are in a logical order and are tied to one another.
   - ○ D. that the reader can hear the writer's voice.

5. When organizing your writing, it is important to
   - ○ A. have good control over the conventions of writing.
   - ○ B. make connections and build bridges.
   - ○ C. polish it for publication.
   - ○ D. argue on a topic about which the writer feels strongly.

6. Which of the following is the purpose of writing to compare/contrast?
   - ○ A. To explain how two things are alike or different
   - ○ B. To explain in detail how to do something
   - ○ C. To discover what caused some effect
   - ○ D. To discover the solution to a problem

7. Which of the following is the purpose of writing to solve a problem?
   - ○ A. To explain how two things are alike or different
   - ○ B. To explain in detail how to do something
   - ○ C. To discover what caused some effect
   - ○ D. To discover the solution to a problem

Name: _____ Date: _____

Unit 2: Writing Skills Test (cont.)

8. Which of the following is the purpose of cause-and-effect writing?
   - ○ A. To explain how two things are alike or different
   - ○ B. To explain in detail how to do something
   - ○ C. To discover what caused some effect
   - ○ D. To discover the solution to a problem

9. Which of the following is the purpose of writing a how-to essay?
   - ○ A. To explain how two things are alike or different
   - ○ B. To explain in detail how to do something
   - ○ C. To discover what caused some effect
   - ○ D. To discover the solution to a problem

10. Writers can elaborate on their instructions by adding all but which one of the following?
    - ○ A. Detailed description
    - ○ B. Location of supplies or materials
    - ○ C. Negative directions
    - ○ D. A headline that states the main idea of the instructions

11. Writing that compares and contrasts leads to more thoughtful decision-making.
    - ○ True   ○ False

12. A cause is something that *makes* something else happen; an effect is the thing that happens.
    - ○ True   ○ False

13. Writing to solve a problem requires finding facts and information.
    - ○ True   ○ False

14. An outline is a sequence of events for writing a report.
    - ○ True   ○ False

15. All but one of these is important when filling out a form. Which one is <u>not</u>?
    - ○ A. Always check to see if the information given is correct.
    - ○ B. Different forms require different information.
    - ○ C. Always check with a parent or guardian before giving out information.
    - ○ D. Organize the information before giving it out.

16. Which of the following statements <u>best</u> describes writing a research report?
    - ○ A. A good research report begins with an interesting question.
    - ○ B. A good research report tells exactly what the source says.
    - ○ C. A good research report is boring.
    - ○ D. A good research report is long, typed, and full of facts.

Name: _____ Date: _____

Unit 2: Writing Skills Test (cont.)

17. Writing Sample: **Comparing Two Relatives**

- Write a paragraph (or paragraphs) in which you compare two close relatives in your family (e.g., your mother with your father or your mother with your grandmother, etc.). Write about the similarities and differences between them.

- Before you begin writing, use scratch paper to organize your ideas.

- Use the best English you can, but do not worry about mistakes. The most important thing is to be clear and organized so the person reading your writing can understand the differences between the two people you selected. Your writing will be evaluated especially for organization.

_____

_____

_____

_____

_____

_____

_____

_____

_____

_____

_____

_____

_____

_____

_____

_____

Unit 3: Writing to Influence—Persuasive Writing

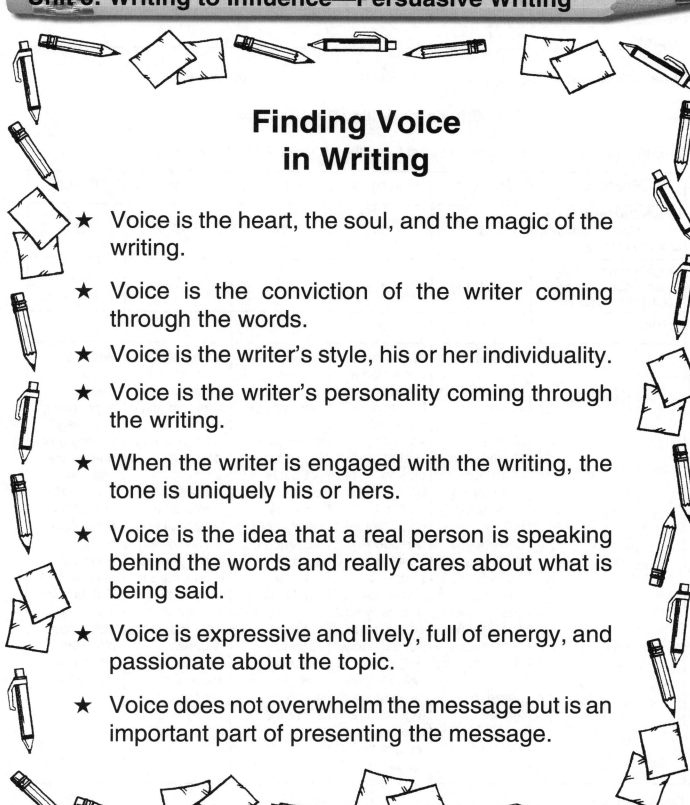

Finding Voice in Writing

★ Voice is the heart, the soul, and the magic of the writing.

★ Voice is the conviction of the writer coming through the words.

★ Voice is the writer's style, his or her individuality.

★ Voice is the writer's personality coming through the writing.

★ When the writer is engaged with the writing, the tone is uniquely his or hers.

★ Voice is the idea that a real person is speaking behind the words and really cares about what is being said.

★ Voice is expressive and lively, full of energy, and passionate about the topic.

★ Voice does not overwhelm the message but is an important part of presenting the message.

Name: _____   Date: _____

Unit 3: Teacher Evaluation Writing Rubric—Voice

Topic: _____

Type of Writing: *Expository*   *Persuasive*   *Narrative*

Criteria for Writing Rubric—Voice

Directions: Circle the number that best describes the quality of the writing.

Features	Not yet	Emerging	Developing	Competent	Strong
Ideas/Content: Is the content focused, original, and interesting?	1	2	3	4	5
Organization: Is the organization clear and helpful to the reader?	1	2	3	4	5
Voice:	1	2	3	4	5
	Writer can't be heard behind the words. Writing lacks purpose; writer doesn't know audience, or text is inappropriate for audience. Writing is "voiceless" and lacks spark, flair, energy, and enthusiasm. Writer seems unsure, bored, or anxious about the topic.	Writer is beginning to communicate; is vaguely aware of audience. Hint of the person behind the words, but often "voice" is hidden more than revealed. Some sparks of energy and enthusiasm, but definitely not consistent. Communication is functional and doesn't involve the reader.	Writer sincerely wants to communicate with the reader. Writer hasn't found "voice" yet but is looking for it. Writer is clear about audience but doesn't address it yet. Writing lacks passion but has sudden bursts of enthusiasm and/or spontaneity.	Writer's voice is clear and unmistakable. Writer is fully aware of audience and communicates in an earnest and personable way. Writer is involved with the topic and works hard to involve the reader. Writer can and does surprise, amuse, or move the reader.	Writer's voice is clear, expressive, and lively. Writing has energy and passion. Tone and voice fit topic, purpose, and audience well. Text is open and honest. Voice does not overwhelm the message.

Comments: _____

_____

36

Name: _____   Date: _____

Unit 3: Student Writing Rubric—Voice

Topic: _____

Type of Writing: *Expository*   *Persuasive*   *Narrative*

Directions: Check those statements that apply to your writing.

_____   I have a clear and interesting topic.

_____   The reader can tell I like this topic.

_____   My writing has pizazz, spark, and personality.

_____   My writing has energy, enthusiasm, and confidence.

_____   My writing sounds like me.

_____   I am open and honest about my topic.

_____   My language is appropriate to my topic and my audience.

_____   I use dialogue in a natural way.

_____   My story reads well out loud.

_____   My writing reaches out to "grab" my reader's attention and holds it right up to the end.

Comments: _____

_____

_____

_____

_____

_____

_____

Name: _____ Date: _____

Unit 3: Writing a Testimonial 1

Key Ideas

- A **testimonial** is a recommendation for a product or service, such as an athlete's testimonial for a certain athletic shoe.

- The purpose of a **testimonial** is to persuade buyers that a particular product or service is the best.

Practice

Directions: Think of a specific product that you use and really like (e.g., your favorite soda or video system). Imagine that the manufacturer of this product asks you for a testimonial of at least 50 words, telling how and why you like the product so much. Write it on the lines below, and be sure to include facts as well as your opinions. Use your own paper if you need more room.

_____

_____

_____

_____

_____

_____

_____

_____

_____

_____

_____

_____

_____

On Your Own: Keep a sharp eye and ear out for advertisements. Usually they contain many opinions but few facts. See if you can find some examples for class discussion.

Name: _____ Date: _____

Unit 3: Writing a Testimonial 2

Key Ideas

- **A testimonial** is a statement recommending a person, product, or service.

- The purpose of **a testimonial** is to persuade the audience of the merits of this person, product, or service.

Practice

Directions: During the many years we spend in school, all of us have our favorite teachers. Sometimes in our busy lives, we don't always take the time to tell them so. Take this opportunity to write a testimonial for a special teacher of yours, nominating him or her for Teacher of the Year.

1. What are some of his or her special characteristics? _____

_____

_____

_____

2. How is he or she different from other teachers you've had? _____

_____

_____

_____

3. What did you learn from this teacher? What did others learn? _____

_____

_____

_____

4. Can you think of a couple of specific examples that illustrate this teacher's special qualities? Describe them.

_____

_____

_____

_____

_____

Name: _____ Date: _____

Unit 3: Writing a Testimonial 2 (cont.)

5. Now that you've brainstormed some ideas, write your first draft of your testimonial to this teacher.

_____

_____

_____

_____

_____

_____

_____

_____

_____

_____

_____

_____

_____

_____

_____

_____

_____

_____

_____

On Your Own: Share your draft with a friend for comments and suggestions on how to improve your writing. Revise your persuasive essay, and then edit and polish it for publication. Teacher of the Year nominations are frequently solicited from local newspapers, TV and radio stations, the Walt Disney Corporation, and some office supply stores. Keep your eyes open for a publishing avenue for your testimonial.

Name: _____ Date: _____

Unit 3: Writing With Voice

Key Ideas

- Your **voice** puts your personal imprint on your writing.

- **Voice** means choosing strong, expressive words for your writing.

- **Voice** means using descriptive language and details to show your feelings and your opinions.

- Writers let their **voice** come through their writing by using familiar words that say just what they mean.

Practice

Directions: Practice writing with voice by completing the exercises below.

Example: *Sentence:*   *Bobbie cried.*
            How?   *Bobbie cried loudly and angrily.*
            Where?   *Bobbie cried loudly and angrily in the nurse's office.*
            When?   *Bobbie cried loudly and angrily for hours after the nurse administered the shot.*

1. Katie escaped.

   How? _____

   _____

   When? _____

   _____

   Where? _____

   _____

2. Yasmine walked.

   How? _____

   _____

   When? _____

   _____

   Where? _____

   _____

3. Roland looked.

   How? _____

   _____

   When? _____

   _____

   Where? _____

   _____

4. Rhonda smiled.

   How? _____

   _____

   When? _____

   _____

   Where? _____

   _____

On Your Own: Practice choosing interesting words to "punch up" your writing. Avoid overly-difficult language, however.

Name: _____ Date: _____

Unit 3: Writing With Voice—Using Strong Verbs

Key Ideas
- Your **voice** puts your personal imprint on your writing.

- When you write, you use **verbs** to tell about actions.
  Example: *played, conquered, ignored, visited, danced*

- When you write, avoid using "overused" verbs like *said.*
  Example: *said = replied, asked, whispered, begged, muttered*

Practice

1. Replace each of these "overworked" verbs with a stronger active verb. Use your thesaurus.

   know   _____   live   _____

   found   _____   work   _____

   run   _____   take   _____

   cut   _____   do   _____

   tell   _____   go   _____

2. Replace each underlined verb with a stronger action verb in each sentence.

   a. The thief <u>ran</u> out of the market with the bread under his arm.

   _____

   _____

   b. The bell <u>rang</u> without warning and scared everyone within listening distance.

   _____

   _____

   c. The policeman <u>walked</u> toward the accident with his gun drawn.

   _____

   _____

Name: _____ Date: _____

Unit 3: Writing a Persuasive Essay

Key Ideas

- **A persuasive essay** is an essay in which the writer argues on a topic he/she has strong beliefs about.

- In **a persuasive essay** the writer introduces his/her argument, presents supporting reasons, draws conclusions, and convinces the reader to accept the writer's viewpoint.

- **A great persuasive essay** has the following characteristics:
  - A clear statement of the writer's position, what he/she wants the reader to believe;
  - At least three strong reasons that support the argument;
  - Elaboration of each argument with facts and examples;
  - Convincing language that is both positive and polite;
  - Clear organization that best persuades the reader;
  - Objections that may be raised by readers are addressed and answered; and
  - The argument and reasons are again summarized at the end of the essay.

Practice

Directions: Is it better to be a boy or a girl in today's society? Why? Write a persuasive essay in which you argue your position, present supporting reasons, and draw conclusions. Remember, the purpose of your essay is to convince your readers or listeners.

1. Explore your argument by creating a diagram like the one below.

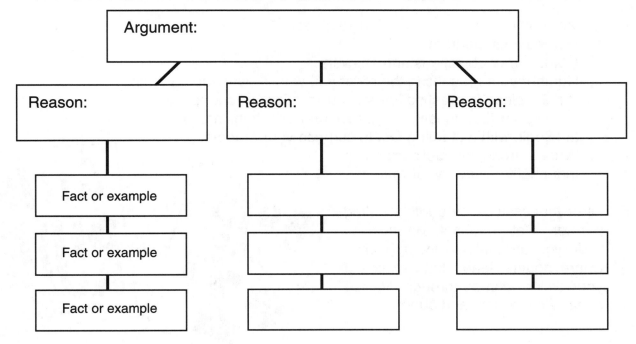

Name: _____ Date: _____

Unit 3: Writing a Persuasive Essay (cont.)

2. Now think of two or three objections that your classmates might have with your argument: "It is better to be a boy/girl in today's society."

   Objection #1: _____

   _____

   Objection #2: _____

   _____

   Objection #3: _____

   _____

3. Think of convincing answers to each of these objections. You may need to find new reasons or new facts and examples.

   Answer to #1: _____

   _____

   Answer to #2: _____

   _____

   Answer to #3: _____

   _____

4. Organize your argument, and plan your essay.
   a. Reread your diagram.
   b. Reread your objections and answers.
   c. Number your reasons in the order you want to write about them.
   d. Write a clear, interesting, strong introduction to your essay.
      1. Begin with a question to get your readers thinking; or
      2. Begin with a startling fact to surprise your readers.
   e. Write a strong, forceful conclusion that briefly reviews your reasons.

5. Draft your essay. Share with a writing partner. Get feedback on how to make your argument stronger. Revise. Share again. Read aloud to see if your "voice" comes through. Revise again. Edit, polish, and publish.

Name: _____ Date: _____

Unit 3: Writing a Persuasive Letter

Key Ideas
- A **persuasive letter** is a letter in which the writer attempts to persuade the reader to do something or to stop doing something.

- There are three basic ways **to persuade people**:
  - Appeal to **reason** (e.g., giving them good, solid reasons for your argument);
  - Appeal to **character** (e.g., find someone they trust and use that person or the reputation of that person to support your argument);
  - Appeal to **emotions** (e.g., concern for their well-being, sense of responsibility, etc.).

Practice

Directions: Whenever we see a really good movie or read a fantastic book, we try to persuade someone else to see it or read it. Write a friendly letter to someone you know well in which you try to persuade him/her to see the movie or read the book. Remember the three basic ways to persuade people listed above.

1. Identify the goal: to see (or read) _____

2. Three good reasons for doing this: _____

   _____

   _____

   _____

3. Possible objections your reader will raise for not doing this: _____

   _____

   _____

   _____

4. Answers to those objections: _____

   _____

   _____

   _____

5. On your own paper, write a strong beginning paragraph, and then write a great concluding paragraph.

6. On your own paper, draft your letter. Share with a writing partner and get feedback. Revise.

Name: _____ Date: _____

Unit 3: Writing a Business Letter

Key Ideas

- **A business letter** is a letter written to a person the writer does not know.

- The purpose of **a business letter** is to request information, to express an opinion, to order a product, or to persuade someone to do something.

- The parts of **a business letter** are a(n):
  - **heading**, which includes the writer's address and date;
  - **inside address**, which is the name and address of the reader;
  - **greeting**, which is followed by a colon (:) rather than a comma (,);
  - **body**, which makes the request or expresses the opinion;
  - **closing**, which is usually more formal (e.g., *cordially, sincerely,* etc.) than in a friendly letter; and
  - **signature**, which includes both a typed and a written signature.

Practice

Directions: Think of the person you would most like to come to your school for an assembly. It could be an author, an actor, or an accountant. Use the chart below to help you organize and plan a business letter to this person persuading him/her to visit your school.

Think:	What is my purpose for writing? Who is my audience?
Plan:	Make notes about what I want to say. Use the tactics I've learned for persuasive writing. Organize my ideas.
Write:	Draft my persuasive letter. Be brief and clear. Use formal language (not slang).
Revise:	With help and suggestions from others, revise my letter so that it is clear and persuasive.
Proof:	Check for mechanical errors. Is my grammar correct? Spelling correct? Punctuation correct? Have I included all six parts of the business letter format?
Publish:	Make a neat, handwritten copy, or type it on a computer or word processor. Add my signature. Address an envelope, stamp, and mail.

On Your Own: Write a letter to request something that you would like to receive. It might be an autographed picture from a performer, a catalog, video refund, etc. Use the business letter format.

Name: _____ Date: _____

Unit 3: Writing an Editorial

Key Ideas

- **An editorial** is a piece of persuasive writing intended to influence readers to the writer's viewpoint.

- **An editorial** has the following parts:
  - A **beginning** that states the writer's position or opinion;
  - A **middle** that contains at least three reasons for the writer's position or opinion; and
  - An **end** that concludes the writing with a personal statement, a prediction, or a summary of the position.

Practice

Directions: Your school board is considering making the school day longer. Write an editorial for your school newspaper persuading the board to vote for or against this proposal. Remember to include all the necessary parts of an editorial.

_____

_____

_____

_____

_____

_____

_____

_____

_____

_____

_____

_____

_____

On Your Own: Write an editorial for your local newspaper persuading people to pass a law requiring people to recycle.

Name: _____ Date: _____

Unit 3: Writing Skills Test

Directions: Darken the circle next to the choice that is the <u>best</u> answer.

1. Writing with voice means
   - ○ A. letting the reader's personality come through the writing.
   - ○ B. letting the writer's personality come through the writing.
   - ○ C. letting the writing do the talking.
   - ○ D. letting the writer's words overpower the message.

2. Finding voice in your writing is important because
   - ○ A. it expands and clarifies the reader's ideas.
   - ○ B. it makes use of colorful, interesting words.
   - ○ C. it is the heart, the soul, and the magic of writing.
   - ○ D. it makes it easy to read the writing.

3. When a piece of reading has "voice" it means
   - ○ A. the reader can sense the real person behind the words.
   - ○ B. the reader can sense that the person behind the words believes in those words.
   - ○ C. the reader can sense that the writer really cares about what is being said.
   - ○ D. all of the above.

4. Writing with voice is important in persuasive writing because
   - ○ A. it uses persuasive writing tools effectively.
   - ○ B. it presents strong arguments and opinions.
   - ○ C. it can persuade the reader to change his/her opinion.
   - ○ D. it helps the writer state his/her position clearly.

5. Which of the following are characteristics of voice?
   - ○ A. The writer is open and honest about the topic.
   - ○ B. The writing sounds like the writer talking.
   - ○ C. The reader can tell the writer likes the topic.
   - ○ D. All of the above

6. Which of the following is the purpose of writing to persuade?
   - ○ A. To chronicle events in one's life or in the lives of others
   - ○ B. To draw generalizations about life
   - ○ C. To learn and share information
   - ○ D. To convince someone to share or accept the writer's way of thinking

7. Which of the following <u>best</u> describes a persuasive letter?
   - ○ A. A letter in which the writer attempts to persuade the reader to do something or to stop doing something
   - ○ B. An essay in which the writer argues on a topic he/she has strong beliefs about
   - ○ C. A letter written to request information, express an opinion, or order a product, etc.
   - ○ D. A recommendation for a product or service

Name: _____ Date: _____

Unit 3: Writing Skills Test (cont.)

8. Which of the following best describes a testimonial?
   - ○ A. A letter in which the writer attempts to persuade the reader to do something or to stop doing something
   - ○ B. An essay in which the writer argues on a topic he/she has strong beliefs about
   - ○ C. A letter written to request information, express an opinion, or order a product, etc.
   - ○ D. A recommendation for a product or service

9. Which of the following best describes a business letter?
   - ○ A. A letter in which the writer attempts to persuade the reader to do something or to stop doing something
   - ○ B. An essay in which the writer argues on a topic he/she has strong beliefs about
   - ○ C. A letter written to request information, express an opinion, or order a product, etc.
   - ○ D. A recommendation for a product or service

10. Which of the following best describes a persuasive essay?
    - ○ A. A letter in which the writer attempts to persuade the reader to do something or to stop doing something
    - ○ B. An essay in which the writer argues on a topic he/she has strong beliefs about
    - ○ C. A letter written to request information, express an opinion, or order a product, etc.
    - ○ D. A recommendation for a product or service

11. Which of these is true of writing with voice?
    - ○ A. Writers use familiar words that say just what they mean.
    - ○ B. Writers use big and difficult words to "punch up" their writing.
    - ○ C. Writers use convincing language to persuade the reader
    - ○ D. Writers use overworked verbs because they are familiar to readers.

12. All but one of these is part of a business letter. Which is not?
    - ○ A. Heading
    - ○ B. Conclusion
    - ○ C. Inside address
    - ○ D. Signature

13. Which of the following words is an example of an "overworked" verb?
    - ○ A. stride
    - ○ B. pace
    - ○ C. walk
    - ○ D. tread

14. Which of the following words is an example of an "overworked" verb?
    - ○ A. tutor
    - ○ B. instruct
    - ○ C. educate
    - ○ D. teach

15. Which of the following best describes the purpose of a testimonial?
    - ○ A. To persuade readers to agree with our opinions
    - ○ B. To persuade buyers that a particular product or service is the best
    - ○ C. To express an opinion
    - ○ D. To agree or disagree with someone or some position

Name: _____ Date: _____

Unit 3: Writing Skills Test (cont.)

16. Writing Sample: **The Power of TV**

- Write a persuasive essay about the influence (if any) that TV has on young people. Do kids get bad/good ideas from watching TV? Can watching TV make them do things they wouldn't otherwise do? Is the influence of TV good or bad on young people? Why?

- Before you begin writing, use scratch paper to organize your ideas. It is important that you introduce your subject clearly and present supporting arguments and reasons.

- Use the best English you can, but do not worry about mistakes. The most important thing is that you convince the reader to agree with your opinion. Your writing will be evaluated especially for voice.

_____

_____

_____

_____

_____

_____

_____

_____

_____

_____

_____

_____

_____

_____

_____

_____

_____

Unit 4: Writing to Entertain or Create—Narrative and Creative Writing

Word Choice in Writing

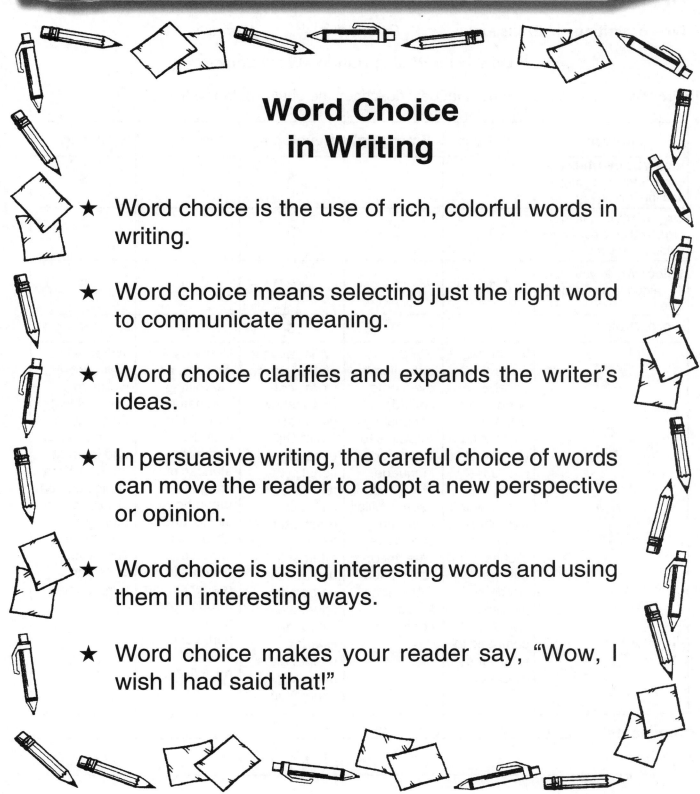

★ Word choice is the use of rich, colorful words in writing.

★ Word choice means selecting just the right word to communicate meaning.

★ Word choice clarifies and expands the writer's ideas.

★ In persuasive writing, the careful choice of words can move the reader to adopt a new perspective or opinion.

★ Word choice is using interesting words and using them in interesting ways.

★ Word choice makes your reader say, "Wow, I wish I had said that!"

Name: _____ Date: _____

Unit 4: Teacher Evaluation Writing Rubric—Word Choice

Topic: _____

Type of Writing: *Expository*   *Persuasive*   *Narrative*

Criteria for Writing Rubric—Word Choice

Directions: Circle the number that best describes the quality of the writing.

Features	Not yet	Emerging	Developing	Competent	Strong
Ideas/Content: Is the content focused, original, and interesting?	1	2	3	4	5
Organization: Is the organization clear and helpful to the reader?	1	2	3	4	5
Voice: Would you read this aloud to someone else?	1	2	3	4	5
Word Choice:	1	2	3	4	5
	Writer has limited vocabulary; word choice is flat, incorrect, or uninteresting. Uses "tired," vague words and phrases and/or clichés. Misuses words and phrases. Reader is confused as to writer's message.	Writer struggles to overcome limited vocabulary. Attempts to use colorful language. More often uses familiar words to communicate. Incorrectly used words lead to reader confusion.	Writer almost always uses words correctly, showing a little "flair." Still uses functional, familiar language most often. Some attempt to use action verbs and figurative language. Reader understands but is not impressed.	Writer uses words in an interesting and natural way. Writing includes some instances of imagery, metaphor, simile, and/or alliteration. Creates pictures in reader's mind through use of active verbs and colorful adjectives.	Writer uses well-chosen words to communicate message in clear, precise, and interesting way. Word choice can be vivid and memorable. Vocabulary suits audience and purpose well.

Comments: _____

_____

Name: _____ Date: _____

Unit 4: Student Writing Rubric—Word Choice

Topic: _____

Type of Writing: *Expository*   *Persuasive*   *Narrative*

Directions: Check those statements that apply to your piece of writing.

_____   I have used many interesting words in my writing; I have used words that I *like*.

_____   I chose just the right words to express my ideas and feelings.

_____   I used phrases and words that are colorful and lively.

_____   I chose words that help the reader see, feel, and understand my message.

_____   I have used everyday words well and some everyday words in new and surprising ways.

_____   My words show action, energy, and/or movement.

_____   I used words that clearly convey feelings.

_____   My story reads well out loud.

_____   My readers will be clear about what my words mean.

Comments: _____

_____

_____

_____

_____

_____

_____

_____

Name: _____ Date: _____

Unit 4: Word Choice

Key Ideas
- One characteristic of good writing is **interesting words**; good writers avoid using "tired" words.

    Example: The <u>boy</u> was <u>happy</u> when he saw the <u>pretty</u> floats in the parade.
    boy   =   youth, youngster, strapling, lad, sprig
    happy =   ecstatic, delighted, elated, jubilant
    pretty =   beautiful, lovely, attractive, gorgeous

    The <u>youngster</u> was <u>elated</u> when he saw the <u>gorgeous</u> floats in the parade.

- A good way to avoid "tired, overused" words and replace them with more interesting ones is to use a thesaurus.

Practice

Directions: For each of these common words, find at least three synonyms that are more interesting. Use a thesaurus or www.websterthesaurus.com on the Internet.

1. mad _____

2. big _____

3. cry _____

4. old _____

5. good _____

6. happy _____

7. fast _____

8. great _____

9. look _____

10. hate _____

On Your Own: Use some of these more interesting words in your writing.

Name: _____ Date: _____

Unit 4: More Word Choice

Key Ideas
- One characteristic of good writing is interesting words; good writers choose **interesting verbs** that "show, not tell."

   Example: *went = scurried, lumbered, sauntered, ambled*
   said = gasped, growled, whined, thundered

- Carefully selected **adverbs** are also a characteristic of good writing.

   Example: *The swan swam <u>lazily</u> across the pond.*
   The man slept <u>fitfully</u> after his nightmare.

Practice

Directions: For each of the verbs below, write at least three more interesting synonyms.

1. take _____

2. show _____

3. run _____

4. look _____

5. move _____

Now choose one of the synonyms for each word above and add an interesting adverb.

   Example: *move = scurry = scurried quickly*

6. take _____ _____

7. show _____ _____

8. run _____ _____

9. look _____ _____

10. move _____ _____

On Your Own: Write some sentences using your interesting verbs and adverbs.

Name: _____ Date: _____

Unit 4: Sensory Poems

Key Ideas

- **Poetry** is a way for authors to express personal feelings and thoughts.

- **Sensory poems** help connect emotions and senses.
    Example: *Noise, confusion, turkey roasting …*

Practice

Directions: Using the following heuristic as a guideline, write a sensory poem about a favorite place.

My Favorite Place
1. Where do you most like to be—of all the places in the world?
2. When do you most like to be there (time and kind of day)?
3. What do you see when you are there?
4. What do you hear when you are there?
5. What do you smell when you are there?
6. What do you do when you are there?
7. Who is there with you?
8. How do you feel when you are there?
9. When will you go there again?

_____

_____

_____

_____

_____

_____

_____

_____

_____

_____

Name: _____ Date: _____

Unit 4: Cinquains

Key Ideas

- **Poetry** is a way for authors to express personal feelings and thoughts.

- **A cinquain** is a structured poem with five unrhymed lines of verse. The format for a **cinquain** is as follows:

> Line 1 - noun
> Line 2 - two adjectives describing the noun
> Line 3 - three verbs showing the action of the noun
> Line 4 - a four-word statement about the noun
> Line 5 - repeats the noun or a synonym for the noun.

Example: *Bubba*
Lively, sweet
Running, jumping, kissing
He loves his people
Puppy.

Practice

Directions: Now you try to write a cinquain here. Be sure to use interesting words to describe and show action.

_____

_____

_____

_____

_____

_____

_____

Once you understand the basic idea, use your thesaurus to replace "tired" words with more interesting words. Keep revising it until you get a poem that you really like.

On Your Own: Keep your eyes and ears open for an idea for a cinquain that is really "out of the ordinary."

Name: _____ Date: _____

Unit 4: Limericks

Key Ideas

- **Poetry** is a way for authors to express personal feelings and thoughts.

- **A limerick** is a form of light verse that uses both rhyme and rhythm.

  A limerick consists of five lines. The first, second, and fifth lines rhyme, while the third and fourth lines rhyme with each other and are shorter than the other three lines. Often the last line contains a funny or surprise ending.

  Example: *There once was a boy named Bob*
                  Who dressed like a slipshod slob
                  He wore no belt
                  And everyone felt
                  That they should just call him "Blob."

Practice

Directions: Working together in small groups, compose a limerick. Use a rhyming dictionary, if needed.

_____

_____

_____

_____

_____

_____

_____

_____

_____

_____

On Your Own: Limericks were popularized by Edward Lear (1812–1888) in England, and collections of his limericks are easily found in libraries. Arnold Lobel has written a book of pig limericks called *Pigericks* that should be available in most school libraries. Check them out!

Name: _____ Date: _____

Unit 4: Clerihews

Key Ideas

- **Poetry** is a way for authors to express personal feelings and thoughts.

- **A clerihew** (KLER-i-hyoo) is a four-line rhymed verse that describes a person.
  The formula for a clerihew is:
  Line 1:   the person's name
  Line 2:   rhymes with the first line
  Line 3 and 4: rhyme with each other

Example: *Britney Spears*
         Accepts the cheers.
         She sings and dances best.
         That is how she won the rest.

Practice

Directions: A clerihew can be written about anyone—a historical figure, fictional characters, real people, yourself, your teacher, or a classmate. With a partner, make up a clerihew. Work on choosing interesting words for your poem.

_____

_____

_____

_____

_____

_____

_____

_____

_____

_____

On Your Own: Clerihews are named for Edmund Clerihew Bentley (1875–1956), an English writer of detective stories who invented this type of poem. Look for other unusual forms of poetry for class discussion.

Unit 4: Writing to Entertain or Create—Narrative and Creative Writing

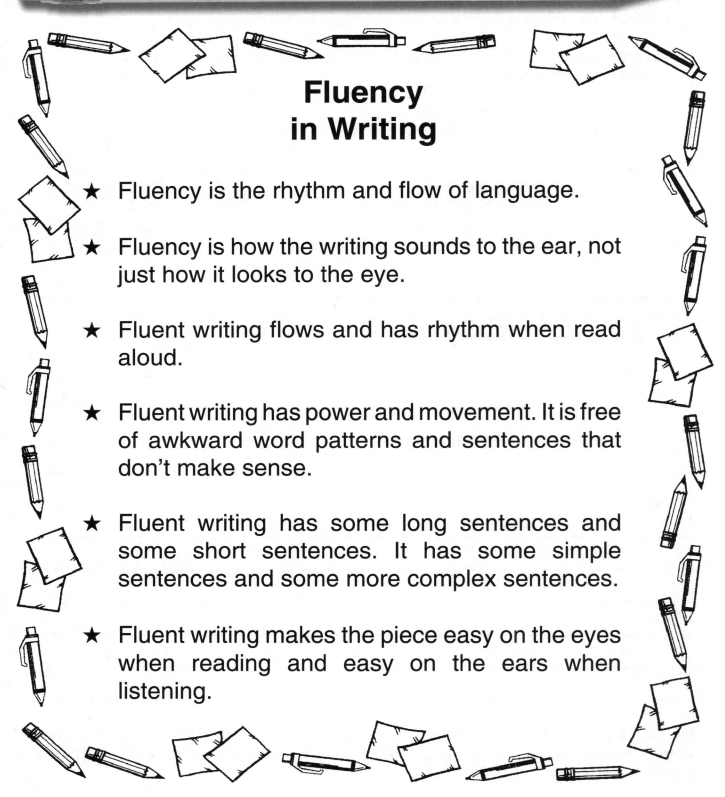

Fluency in Writing

★ Fluency is the rhythm and flow of language.

★ Fluency is how the writing sounds to the ear, not just how it looks to the eye.

★ Fluent writing flows and has rhythm when read aloud.

★ Fluent writing has power and movement. It is free of awkward word patterns and sentences that don't make sense.

★ Fluent writing has some long sentences and some short sentences. It has some simple sentences and some more complex sentences.

★ Fluent writing makes the piece easy on the eyes when reading and easy on the ears when listening.

Name: _____ Date: _____

Unit 4: Teacher Evaluation Writing Rubric—Fluency

Topic: _____

Type of Writing: *Expository*   *Persuasive*   *Narrative*

Criteria for Writing Rubric—Fluency

Directions: Circle the number that best describes the quality of the writing.

Features	Not yet	Emerging	Developing	Competent	Strong
Ideas/Content: Is the content focused, original, and interesting?	1	2	3	4	5
Organization: Is organization clear and helpful to reader?	1	2	3	4	5
Voice: Would you read this aloud to someone else?	1	2	3	4	5
Word Choice: Do words and phrases create vivid mind pictures?	1	2	3	4	5
Fluency:	1	2	3	4	5
	Writer uses unusual or irregular word patterns. Sentences are short and choppy or long and convoluted. Writing contains run-ons and fragments and is hard to understand. It is difficult to read and understand the message.	Writer has some purposeful sentences and some "sense" of colorful language. Uses repetitive and awkward word patterns. Choppy sentences, run-ons, and fragments make it difficult to read aloud.	Writer attempts to vary length and structure of sentences. Parts of text are easily read aloud, others may be stiff, awkward, or choppy. Sentences are usually grammatically correct but make little use of time clues.	Writer uses sentences that are strong, grammatical, clear, and direct. Variation in sentence length and structure help make meaning clear and interesting. Piece has nice flow or rhythm and is easily read aloud.	Writer constructs sentences that are straightforward, clear, grammatical, and complete. The writing has flow, cadence, and rhythm when read aloud. Sentences vary in length, but most are compact with no wasted words.

Comments: _____

_____

Name: _____ Date: _____

Unit 4: Student Writing Rubric—Fluency

Topic: _____

Type of Writing: *Expository*   *Persuasive*   *Narrative*

Directions: Check those statements that apply to your piece of writing.

_____   My sentences are clear and varied.

_____   My paper has "rhythm" when read aloud; my writing is smooth.

_____   I have used different sentence beginnings; all of my sentences do not begin the same way.

_____   I have written some long sentences and some short sentences.

_____   Some of my sentences are simple, and some are complex.

_____   I used time clues when appropriate.

_____   Every sentence in my paper **is** a sentence; there are no run-on sentences or fragments.

_____   Every sentence is important to the meaning of my paper; there are no unnecessary sentences.

_____   My sentences are concise, not wordy.

_____   My writing is easy for the reader to follow.

Comments: _____

_____

_____

_____

_____

_____

_____

_____

Name: _____ Date: _____

Unit 4: Story Characters 1

Key Ideas

- **A story** is a narrative made up by the author. It may be true, untrue, or partially true.

- **An interesting story** is about interesting characters—usually people or animals we care about.

- Writers develop **story characters** in four ways:
  1. **Appearance** - how characters look
  2. **Action** - what characters do
  3. **Dialogue** - what characters say
  4. **Monologue** - what characters think

- **Details** about characters are important. When you describe a character, choose details that make that person special.

Practice

Directions: Write three character sketches describing real or imagined people in **great** detail. Start with people you know. Look at your parents, your friends' parents, your teachers, your schoolmates, or your neighbors. Look at them as if you have never seen them before. What makes them tick? Are they kind or wise or funny? What are some outstanding details about their appearance? What do they wish for? What are they afraid of? What are some outstanding details about how they sound, speak, or walk? Do they use their hands when they talk? Do they always wear black? Do they chew on their pencils, eat their pizza in a funny way, or twirl their hair nervously?

Don't write about three people who are the same age or have the same background as you. At least one of them should be much older than you and living a different life than you are. Try to imagine what their lives are like. Be creative. Get inside their heads.

1. _____

_____

_____

_____

_____

_____

_____

_____

_____

_____

Name: _____ Date: _____

Unit 4: Story Characters 1 (cont.)

2. _____

_____

_____

_____

_____

_____

_____

_____

_____

_____

_____

3. _____

_____

_____

_____

_____

_____

_____

_____

_____

_____

Name: _____ Date: _____

Unit 4: Story Characters 2

Key Ideas

- **A story** is a narrative made up by the author. It may be true, untrue, or partially true.

- **An interesting story** is about interesting characters—usually people or animals we care about.

- Writers develop **story characters** in four ways:
    1. **Appearance** - how characters look
    2. **Action** - what characters do
    3. **Dialogue** - what characters say
    4. **Monologue** - what characters think

- **A monologue** is a conversation with yourself.

Practice

Directions: Write a short monologue for one of your characters.

    Choose one of the three characters you've just invented. Choose the one that interests you the most—not necessarily the one most like you, but the one who you think you would like to know better. Crawl into that character's head. Talk like that character. A monologue is talking to oneself, so *be* the character talking to himself/herself, reminding himself/herself what he or she dislikes or is crazy about or is puzzled by. Let this monologue tell your readers something about the character. Let it reveal a bad habit, a way of looking at the world, or simply something that annoys or pleases this person. After you've finished the monologue, give it a title.

_____

_____

_____

_____

_____

_____

_____

_____

_____

_____

_____

Name: _____ Date: _____

Unit 4: Story Characters 3

Key Ideas

- **A story** is a narrative made up by the author. It may be true, untrue, or partially true.

- **An interesting story** is about interesting characters—usually people or animals we care about.

- Writers develop **story characters** in four ways:
    1. **Appearance** - how characters look
    2. **Action** - what characters do
    3. **Dialogue** - what characters say
    4. **Monologue** - what characters think

- **A dialogue** is a conversation between two people.

Practice

Directions: Write a short dialogue between two of your characters that represents a huge misunderstanding between them. Again, try to get into the characters' heads and talk the way they talk, act the way they act, and behave the way they would behave. Use play format for your dialogue.

Example: *Marci: But I told you not to do that.*
Mom: What did I do?

_____   _____

_____

_____   _____

_____

_____   _____

_____

_____   _____

Name: _____ Date: _____

Unit 4: Story Setting

Key Ideas

- **A story** is a narrative made up by the author. It may be true, untrue, or partially true.

- The **setting** is where and when the story takes place. The **setting** includes location, weather, time of day, time period, and so on.

- The **setting** can be integral to the story; that is, the setting can play an important part in the story, as in a mystery with a haunted house. The **setting** may also be a backdrop to the action of the story, as in a fairy tale, "In a dark, dark forest" or "In a faraway land."

Practice

Directions: Practice describing the various types of settings listed below. It is important in describing the setting to use interesting word choice and great detail. You want your reader to *see* what you are describing.

1. Describe an indoor setting that you know well.

    _____

    _____

    _____

    _____

    _____

    _____

    _____

2. Describe an outdoor setting that you know well.

    _____

    _____

    _____

    _____

    _____

    _____

    _____

Unit 4: Story Setting (cont.)

3. This time, pretend a mystery has taken place in your indoor setting. Describe it again, changing or adding details to make your reader pay attention and become a detective.

_____

_____

_____

_____

_____

_____

4. Do the same thing now with your outdoor setting. Mystery settings usually include unusual or strange details, so be sure to add some to your description.

_____

_____

_____

_____

_____

_____

_____

5. Now, pick your best setting and have one of your characters enter that setting. Your character may look or act normal, but there is something odd or mysterious about him or her. First introduce the setting, and then introduce the character.

_____

_____

_____

_____

_____

On Your Own: Try writing the opening again using a different character or a different setting. How does it change the story?

Name: _____ Date: _____

Unit 4: Story Plot 1

Key Ideas

- **A story** is a narrative made up by the author. It may be true, untrue, or partially true.

- **The plot** of the story is the sequence of events in a story and is made up of **a beginning**, **a middle**, and **an end**.

- **The beginning** of the story introduces the characters, describes the setting, establishes the problem, and gets the reader interested in the story.

- **The problem** involves a conflict with another person, with nature, or within the character himself/herself.

Practice

Directions: You have already described the setting and introduced the characters. Your task now is to establish the problem. Think of a problem that might fit the situations below.

1. Write about one of your characters who witnesses another of your characters treating someone badly.

   _____

   _____

   _____

   _____

   _____

   _____

2. Write about a small act of violence (e.g., being mugged, being in an accident, facing a bully) happening to one of your characters.

   _____

   _____

   _____

   _____

   _____

   _____

Name: _____ Date: _____

Unit 4: Story Plot 1 (cont.)

3. Write about your characters (one or more) getting trapped by the weather (e.g., tornado, blizzard, hurricane, etc.). What happens to them?

_____

_____

_____

_____

_____

_____

4. Write about one of your characters doing something destructive to himself or herself. He or she knows not to do it but just can't seem to stop.

_____

_____

_____

_____

_____

_____

Directions: These writing assignments illustrate the three types of conflict that occur in stories: **person against person, person against nature, person against self**. Can you identify each example?

1. One character witnessing another character treating someone badly: _____

2. Small act of violence happening to a character: _____

3. Characters being trapped by the weather conditions: _____

4. A character doing something destructive to himself or herself: _____

Name: _____ Date: _____

Unit 4: Story Plot 2

Key Ideas

- **A story** is a narrative made up by the author. It may be true, untrue, or partially true.

- **The plot** of the story is the sequence of events in a story and is made up of **a beginning**, **a middle**, and **an end**.

- **Plot** has four parts:
  1. **A problem** - the problem introduces conflict at the beginning of the story.
  2. **Roadblocks** - characters face roadblocks as they try to solve the problem in the middle of the story.
  3. **Climax** - the high point in the action occurs when the problem is about to be solved. It separates the middle from the end.
  4. **Solution** - The problem is solved, and the roadblocks are overcome at the end of the story.

Practice

Directions: Now that you have the conflict, map out your plot using a chart like the one below.

The Problem	Roadblocks	Climax	Solution
Make trouble for the main character—not too easy (or you won't have anything to write about), not too hard (or you'll be writing all day).	Roadblocks are the things that get in the way of the main character solving the problem. Roadblocks create suspense by making readers wonder if your main character will succeed. Other characters can *help* solve the problem but can't actually solve the problem for the main character.	The high point of the story is when the problem is about to be solved. The climax should be the most suspenseful part of the story.	The problem is solved, and the roadblocks are overcome.

Unit 4: Good Story Beginnings

Key Ideas

- **A story** is a narrative made up by the author. It may be true, untrue, or partially true.

- **The plot** of the story is the sequence of events in a story and is made up of **a beginning**, **a middle**, and **an end**.

- The **beginning** of the story introduces the characters, describes the setting, establishes the problem, and gets the readers interested in the story.

- A good **beginning**:
  - Grabs the reader's attention right away.
  - Might start with a question.
  - Might make a statement that surprises the reader.
  - Might start with a person's words (dialogue).

Practice

Directions: Below are samples of some good beginnings and some weaker beginnings. Read them and discuss the differences between good and weak beginnings. What are some of the ways these authors "grabbed" your attention?

Good beginnings	**Weak** beginnings
1. "I need to leave, I hate it here, I need to get out!" My words rattled the ceiling.	A. When I was a little girl, I hated going to visit my aunt.
2. I met him sailing.	B. My dad and I went sailing one day, and we met Jennings.
3. As I walked through the forest of darkness, I realized one thing—I was alone.	C. My scariest moment was when I got lost in the woods alone.
4. The boat jerked away from the dock and drifted crazily out to sea.	D. One time I was alone in the boat.
5. Once a new girl walked into the classroom.	E. When I moved to my new school, I didn't know anyone.

Name: _____ Date: _____

Unit 4: Good Story Beginnings (cont.)

Directions: Working in small groups, rewrite these weak beginnings.

1. I woke up to a very loud noise really early in the morning.

   _____

   _____

   _____

   _____

2. On the last day of school, we rode our bicycles to the store.

   _____

   _____

   _____

   _____

3. For my birthday this year, we went to Six Flags Amusement Park, and I rode the roller coaster for the first time.

   _____

   _____

   _____

   _____

4. My proudest moment was when I won the 100-yard dash in fourth grade.

   _____

   _____

   _____

   _____

5. One day, my friend Justine and I were walking home from school.

   _____

   _____

   _____

   _____

On Your Own: Take one of your drafts of the beginnings of your story. Rework it, revise it, and rewrite it until you feel it is a strong beginning that introduces the characters, describes the setting, establishes the problem, and "grabs" the reader's attention.

Name: _____ Date: _____

Unit 4: Story Middles

Key Ideas

- **A story** is a narrative made up by the author. It may be true, untrue, or partially true.

- **The plot** of the story is the sequence of events in a story and is made up of **a beginning**, **a middle**, and **an end**.

- The following things happen in the **middle** of a story:
  - The problem gets worse.
  - Roadblocks continually get in the way for the main character.
  - More information is revealed about the characters.
  - The middle is the longest part.
  - Readers really become "hooked" on the story and empathize with the characters and their problems.

Practice

Directions: Using your characters, setting, and conflict, plan the middle of your story here. Show the characters trying to deal with the problem. Add roadblocks and help characters deal with those roadblocks.

_____

_____

_____

_____

_____

_____

_____

_____

_____

_____

_____

On Your Own: Try out your story middle on a classmate. See if he or she has any good suggestions for making your middle stronger or more suspenseful. Revise.

Unit 4: Story Endings

Key Ideas

- **A story** is a narrative made up by the author. It may be true, untrue, or partially true.

- **The plot** of the story is the sequence of events in a story and is made up of **a beginning**, **a middle**, and **an end**.

- The following things happen in the **ending** of a story:
  - The problem is resolved.
  - The loose ends are tied up.
  - Readers feel that the story is finished; they feel satisfied with the ending.

- As with beginnings, there is no one correct way to **end** your story. Try different endings until you find one that makes the story feel finished.

> **Example 1:** My team beat the best soccer team in the region. We won the championship game.

> **Example 2:** I couldn't believe it! We smashed the best boys' soccer team in our area and enjoyed doing it. We were the champs! What an exciting victory that was!

> Which ending sounds "finished"? Both endings tell how the experience worked out, but Example 2 describes how the writer felt about the experience.

Practice

Directions: Below are some endings to stories. Decide if you think they are good endings or weak endings. Be ready to give the reasons for your choice.

1. I finally had a friend and began to fit into the classroom. _____

2. I went home with the worst haircut I have ever had. _____

3. With the crack of the bat, the ball flew toward me in the left field seats. A dozen people reached up to grab it, but it landed in my lap. I couldn't believe it! I had caught a Mark McGwire home run! _____

4. Chin and I worked harder on the project than anyone else. _____

5. It was funny when I put shampoo on it. We laughed and laughed and laughed. And then we had cookies. Then we went to bed. The end. _____

Name: _____ Date: _____

Unit 4: Story Endings (cont.)

6. My friends thought the test was easy. I thought it was hard.   _____
    "Did you read the story?" they asked. "Of course I did." But
    I found out it was the wrong story! I was so upset. I failed the
    test but learned a good lesson. Check your homework more
    than once.

7. I was so smart back in kindergarten and first grade. You know   _____
    what? Some day I'll be a kindergarten or first grade teacher
    myself.

8. Gone, like the bases of the baseball field, gone like chalk lines   _____
    running in the rain. It was time for me to wave good-bye.

9. "Now I know why they call it Raging Rivers," I said to my   _____
    cousin, "I'm soaked to the bone."

10. And then the guard at the zoo made us throw our soda in   _____
    the garbage.

11. Fred was never seen or heard from again. And that's the   _____
    end of my story.

12. But the important thing about my dog is that she is a golden   _____
    retriever.

Directions: Working in small groups, rewrite these weak endings to make them stronger.

1. When he kicked the ball, it landed right in the cake.

    _____

    _____

    _____

2. I didn't say anything, but I did not agree with him.

    _____

    _____

    _____

    _____

Name: _____ Date: _____

Unit 4: Story Endings (cont.)

3. And finally he took me home soaking wet.

_____

_____

_____

4. He walked right into the hole and disappeared.

_____

_____

_____

5. From then on, whenever I played a bad note, my dog would howl.

_____

_____

_____

Directions: Work with your own writing. Practice writing a strong ending to your story. Write at least two different endings to the story. Remember to include the characteristics of a good ending mentioned in the **Key Ideas**.

Ending 1: _____

_____

_____

_____

_____

Ending 2: _____

_____

_____

_____

_____

On Your Own: Which ending do you like best? Why? Does it keep the reader's attention? Does it make the story feel finished? Does it tell how the experience worked out? Does it solve the problem? Are all loose ends tied up? Share it with a partner. See if he or she agrees with your assessment.

Unit 4: Story—Putting It All Together

Key Ideas

- **A story** is a narrative made up by the author. It may be true, untrue, or partially true.
- **Stories** are made up of three parts: **a beginning**, **a middle**, and **an end**.

- Writers put the following things in the **beginning** of the story:
  - The characters are introduced.
  - The setting is described.
  - The problem is established.
  - Readers become interested in the story.

- Writers put the following things in the **middle** of the story:
  - The problem gets worse.
  - Roadblocks continually get in the way of the main character.
  - More information is revealed about the characters.
  - The middle is the longest part.
  - Readers really become "hooked" on the story and empathize with the characters and their problems.

- Writers put the following things in the **end** of the story:
  - The problem gets resolved.
  - The loose ends are tied up.
  - Readers feel satisfied and finished with the story.

Practice

Directions: Now that you have all the bits and pieces of your story written, write your first draft on your own paper. Follow the story map you created on the chart earlier.

| BEGINNING Introduce the characters | MIDDLE Problems and roadblocks | END Problem is resolved |

Name: _____ Date: _____

Unit 4: Writing Skills Test

Directions: Darken the circle next to the choice that is the <u>best</u> answer.

1. Word choice is important in writing because
   - ○ A. selecting the right word helps to communicate meaning.
   - ○ B. it makes the paper more interesting.
   - ○ C. it helps the reader organize the paper.
   - ○ D. it is important for choosing the right format for the audience.

2. Which one of these <u>best</u> represents what careful word choice can do?
   - ○ A. help the reader understand the writer's message
   - ○ B. help the writer communicate the message
   - ○ C. help the writer clarify and expand his/her ideas
   - ○ D. all of the above

3. Another description of word choice is
   - ○ A. using words that show action, energy, and movement.
   - ○ B. using words that show a good vocabulary.
   - ○ C. using words that the writer looked up in a thesaurus.
   - ○ D. using words that the reader probably won't know.

4. Fluency in writing means
   - ○ A. the writer chose just the right words to make sense.
   - ○ B. the writer chose words that rhyme with each other.
   - ○ C. the writer's words have a rhythm and flow to them.
   - ○ D. the writer's sentences are strong and clear.

5. Fluency can be checked by
   - ○ A. counting the number of three-syllable words.
   - ○ B. looking for the sense of the words.
   - ○ C. checking for irregular word patterns.
   - ○ D. listening for the flow and rhythm when read aloud.

6. Which of the following <u>best</u> describes a poem?
   - ○ A. A narrative made up by the author
   - ○ B. A brief word picture
   - ○ C. A play on words to create images or explore ideas
   - ○ D. A drama created for viewing

7. Which of these <u>best</u> describes a *sensory* poem?
   - ○ A. A form that helps connect emotions and senses
   - ○ B. A structured poem with five unrhymed lines of verse
   - ○ C. A form of light verse that uses both rhyme and rhythm
   - ○ D. A four-lined rhymed verse that describes a person

Name: _____ Date: _____

Unit 4: Writing Skills Test (cont.)

8. Which of these <u>best</u> describes a *clerihew*?
   - ○ A. A form that helps connect emotions and senses
   - ○ B. A structured poem with five unrhymed lines of verse
   - ○ C. A form of light verse that uses both rhyme and rhythm
   - ○ D. A four-lined rhymed verse that describes a person

9. Which of these <u>best</u> describes a *limerick*?
   - ○ A. A form that helps connect emotions and senses
   - ○ B. A structured poem with five unrhymed lines of verse
   - ○ C. A form of light verse that uses both rhyme and rhythm
   - ○ D. A four-lined rhymed verse that describes a person

10. Which of these <u>best</u> describes a *cinquain*?
   - ○ A. A form that helps connect emotions and senses
   - ○ B. A structured poem with five unrhymed lines of verse
   - ○ C. A form of light verse that uses both rhyme and rhythm
   - ○ D. A four-lined rhymed verse that describes a person

11. Which of the following <u>best</u> describes a *story*?
   - ○ A. A narrative made up by the author
   - ○ B. A brief word picture
   - ○ C. A play on words to create images or explore ideas
   - ○ D. A drama created for viewing

12. A good story has all but which one of the following?
   - ○ A. A beginning that sets up the plot, the setting, and the characters
   - ○ B. A middle that shows how characters deal with the problem
   - ○ C. A play on words arranged artfully on a page
   - ○ D. An ending that shows how the characters solve the problem

13. Writers develop characters in all but which one of these ways?
   - ○ A. How characters look
   - ○ B. What characters do and say
   - ○ C. What characters think
   - ○ D. What problems characters encounter

14. Which of the following describes the *plot* of a story?
   - ○ A. A conflict with another person, with nature, or within the character
   - ○ B. Where and when the story takes place
   - ○ C. The sequence of events in a story
   - ○ D. Who the story is about

Name: _____ Date: _____

Unit 4: Writing Skills Test (cont.)

15. Which of the following describes the characters of a story?
    ○ A. A conflict with another person, with nature, or within the character
    ○ B. Where and when the story takes place
    ○ C. The sequence of events in a story
    ○ D. Who the story is about

16. Which of the following describes the setting of a story?
    ○ A. A conflict with another person, with nature, or within the character
    ○ B. Where and when the story takes place
    ○ C. The sequence of events in a story
    ○ D. Who the story is about

17. Which of the following describes the problem of a story?
    ○ A. A conflict with another person, with nature, or within the character
    ○ B. Where and when the story takes place
    ○ C. The sequence of events in a story
    ○ D. Who the story is about

18. Which of the following does <u>not</u> represent one of the types of conflicts in a story?
    ○ A. Person against person
    ○ B. Person against self
    ○ C. Person against nature
    ○ D. Person against animal

19. Writers generally put all but one of these things in the middle of their stories:
    ○ A. Roadblocks that frustrate the main character
    ○ B. More information about the characters
    ○ C. The resolution of the problem
    ○ D. The climax of the story

20. Good endings have all but which one of the following?
    ○ A. The reader has feelings of sympathy for the main character.
    ○ B. There is a resolution to the problem.
    ○ C. All loose ends are tied up.
    ○ D. The reader feels satisfied, and the story feels finished.

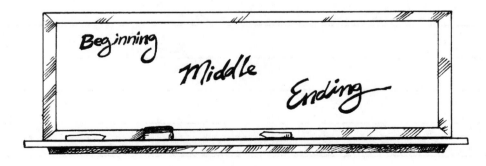

Name: _____ Date: _____

Unit 4: Writing Skills Test (cont.)

21. Writing Sample: **The Wish**

   • Write a story in which a character wishes for something that turns out to be bad for him/
   her when he/she gets the wish. What is the wish?

   • Before you begin writing, use scratch paper to organize your ideas. It is important to use
   your imagination to think up great ideas. Remember to describe interesting characters
   and put them in an engaging setting. Describe the problem and put up roadblocks.
   Resolve the problem in the end.

   • Use the best English you can, but do not worry about mistakes. The most important thing
   is to write clearly so that the person reading your story can imagine what is happening
   from the beginning to the end. Use the notes that you made on the scratch paper to
   remember your ideas and to stay organized. Your writing will be evaluated especially for
   word choice and fluency.

   _____

   _____

   _____

   _____

   _____

   _____

   _____

   _____

   _____

   _____

   _____

   _____

   _____

   _____

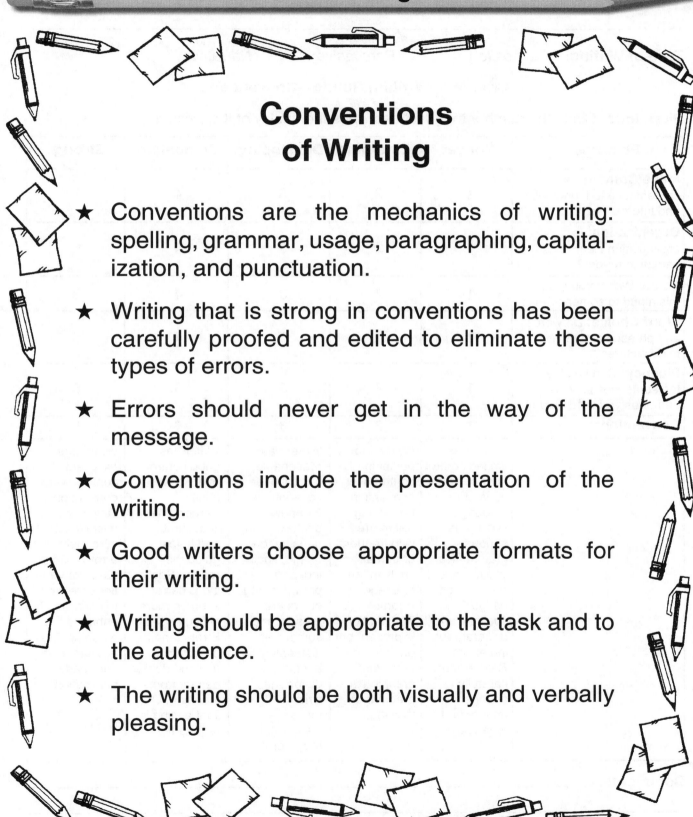

Conventions of Writing

★ Conventions are the mechanics of writing: spelling, grammar, usage, paragraphing, capitalization, and punctuation.

★ Writing that is strong in conventions has been carefully proofed and edited to eliminate these types of errors.

★ Errors should never get in the way of the message.

★ Conventions include the presentation of the writing.

★ Good writers choose appropriate formats for their writing.

★ Writing should be appropriate to the task and to the audience.

★ The writing should be both visually and verbally pleasing.

Name: _____ Date: _____

Section II: Teacher Evaluation Writing Rubric—Conventions

Topic: _____

Type of Writing: *Expository*   *Persuasive*   *Narrative*

Criteria for Writing Rubric—Conventions

Directions: Circle the number that best describes the quality of the writing.

Features	Not yet	Emerging	Developing	Competent	Strong
Ideas/Content: Is content focused, original, and interesting?	1	2	3	4	5
Organization: Is organization clear and helpful to reader?	1	2	3	4	5
Voice: Would you read this aloud to someone else?	1	2	3	4	5
Word Choice: Do words and phrases create vivid mind pictures?	1	2	3	4	5
Fluency: Can you feel the sentences flow together as you read aloud?	1	2	3	4	5
Conventions:	1	2	3	4	5
	Writer has limited control over conventions of language. Writing has serious grammatical, capitalization, punctuation, usage, spelling, and/or paragraphing errors. Reader must carefully decode to understand meaning.	Writer shows beginning control over conventions, but writing is still marred with frequent grammar, spelling, and/or usage errors. Punctuation is present but often incorrect. Paragraphing is irregular or missing.	Writer has reasonable control over conventions. Grammar, capitalization, punctuation, usage, spelling, and paragraphing errors are present and somewhat distracting but do not distort the writer's message. Reads like a rough draft.	Writer has good control over conventions. Paragraphing is accurate and helps guide the reader. Spelling is correct, even on more difficult words. Errors tend to be minor or few and do not detract from meaning. Only light editing is required.	Writer has excellent control over conventions. Only picky mistakes or infrequent errors. Writer uses conventions cleverly to consistently enhance the meaning. Text is clean, clear, and ready for publication.

Comments: _____

_____

Name: _____   Date: _____

Section II: Student Writing Rubric—Conventions

Topic: _____

Type of Writing: *Expository*   *Persuasive*   *Narrative*

Student Writing Rubric: Conventions

Directions: Check those statements that apply to your writing.

_____   My spelling is correct.

_____   My punctuation is correct.

_____   My grammar is correct.

_____   I carefully revised this paper.

_____   I carefully edited this paper.

_____   There are no significant errors in my paper.

_____   My format is appropriate to my audience and for my purpose.

_____   I followed the format given with the assignment.

_____   My paper has a pleasing layout and effective use of white space.

_____   Readers can read my handwriting.

_____   I have a "dy-no-mite" title for my paper.

Comments: _____

_____

_____

_____

_____

_____

_____

Name: _____ Date: _____

Unit 5: Punctuation 1—End Punctuation

Key Ideas

- **A period** always follows a declarative sentence and usually follows an imperative sentence.

    Example: *No one knows for sure who made the first American flag.*
                    Please put the flag away.

- **A question mark** follows an interrogative sentence.

    Example: *Did you see the after-school special on TV yesterday?*

- **An exclamation point** always follows an exclamation and sometimes follows an imperative sentence.

    Example: *Wow, look what I found!*
                    Come here, now!

Practice

Directions: Choose the right punctuation mark, and add it to the end of each of these sentences.

1. Here you are

2. Where were you hiding

3. I bet you were hiding in the closet in the kitchen

4. I couldn't find you anywhere

5. Why didn't you come when I called you

6. You almost frightened me to death

7. Don't ever do that again

8. Now go lie down in your bed by the fireplace and stay there

9. I don't want to have to go looking for you again

10. Understand

On Your Own: Can you write a paragraph using each type of end mark at least twice?

Name: _____ Date: _____

Unit 5: Punctuation 2—Commas

Key Ideas
- **Commas** are used to separate items in a series.
  - **Example:** *She bought a new coat, two sweaters, and a skirt for school.*

- **Commas** are used to set off parenthetic words and expressions—words and expressions that interrupt the sentence.
  - **Example:** *No, I didn't see the movie. I did read the book, however.*

- **Commas** are used to set off the name of a person directly addressed.
  - **Example:** *Quentin, stop making that noise with your shoe.*

Practice

Directions: Using the editor's mark for inserting commas (⌄), place commas in the sentences where they belong. Also place the correct end punctuation at the end of each sentence.

1. When you go out in the snow wear your coat mittens and hat

2. Preston did you hear what I said

3. This child I swear would go out in this frigid weather without a coat if I let him

4. Margaret did you notice that last night it rained snowed and thundered

5. Wow What odd weather we are having don't you think

6. What is going on with the weather I wonder

7. In this month alone we have had hot weather cold weather rainy weather and sunny

    weather

8. Randall of course enjoyed the weather variety

9. How does he stand all the changes Marie

10. Preston wear your boots

On Your Own: Write a sentence that illustrates all three uses of commas described above. Leave out the commas and give to a friend to see if he/she can correctly insert the commas.

87

Name: _____ Date: _____

Unit 5: Punctuation 3—More Commas

Key Ideas

- **A comma** is used to separate two independent clauses (that is, two clauses that *could* stand alone as sentences) linked by a coordinate conjunction (e.g., *and, but, or, nor, yet*).
    Example: *Leonardo bought the tickets, and Maria rented the car.*

- **Commas** are used to set off modifying phrases and clauses when they come before the main clause.
    Example: *Falling down the stairs, she dropped all her books.*

- **Commas** are used to separate two or more coordinate, or equal, adjectives.
    Example: *The hot, thirsty players drank lots of water during the game.*

Practice

Directions: Using the editor's mark for inserting commas (⋏), place commas in the sentences where they belong.

1. To win she worked very hard.

2. Under a tree in the hammock my father slept.

3. Kamal is a tall handsome young man.

4. Santa delivered the toys and Mrs. Santa made the

    cookies.

5. When I returned from camp my room was no longer the same.

6. Today was a hot sunny day.

7. Penny brought the blanket and Dylan brought the flashlight.

8. To go on the field trip Thomas had to sell 14 boxes of cookies.

9. We played well and we were happy.

10. Edward is a loud boisterous player.

On Your Own: Make up five sentences of your own following one of the comma rules. Omit the commas from your sentences. Trade with a partner and have him/her insert the commas where they belong. Using the key ideas at the top of this page, check the sentences.

88

Name: _____ Date: _____

Unit 5: Punctuation 4—Italics and Underlining

Key Ideas

- The titles of books, long poems, plays, movies, pieces of art, long pieces of music, magazines, and newspapers are italicized (or underlined in handwriting).
  Examples: My favorite book is *The Raging Quiet* by Sheryl Jordan.
  Elton John was on the cover of *Rolling Stone* magazine.

- The names of ships, planes, and spacecraft are also italicized (underlined).
  Example: The captain and 14-man crew of the British ship the *Mary Celeste* disappeared in 1872 and have never been found.

- Words used as words and letters used as letters within a sentence are italicized (or underlined).
  Examples: There are two *r*'s in the word *tomorrow*.
  Kalli misspelled the word *extemporaneous* in the spelling bee.

Practice

Direction: Think of an example of each of the following items, and write it on the line. Be sure to underline each of your examples if it is necessary.

1. Name of a book: _____

2. Name of a magazine: _____

3. Name of a comic book: _____

4. Name of a movie: _____

5. Name of a movie star: _____

6. Name of an opera: _____

7. Name of a singer: _____

8. Name of a newspaper: _____

9. Name of a work of art: _____

10. Name of a composer: _____

11. Name of a play: _____

12. Name of an author: _____

Name: _____ Date: _____

Unit 5: Punctuation 5—Colons

Key Ideas
- **A colon** is used to introduce a list.
  - **Example:** *Please send the following items: apples, pears, and bananas.*

- **A colon** can also be used to introduce an explanation, an example, or a quotation.
  - **Examples:** *She has but one goal: success.*

    Only one task remains: to take her final exams.

    To be successful, do the following: stay in school, study, and participate in extra-curricular activities.

    Shakespeare said: "To be or not to be ..."

Practice

Directions: Edit the following sentences, inserting colons where needed. Use the editor's mark for inserting colons (⋏).

1. The first chore assigned to me at camp laundry.

2. One thing is certain The new person at camp always has to do the worst job.

3. Given the terrible weather of the last few days, I was relieved by what was coming nice, sunny, dry days.

4. I strode up to the dozens of washing machines in the laundry and quoted John Paul Jones "I have not yet begun to fight."

5. Finally, I got to participate in the activities I came for games, swimming, and riding.

6. There were children of many different nationalities at camp this year American, Asian, English, German, Spanish, and French.

7. There is one lesson I learned at camp Everyone is basically the same.

8. During the last week, we participated in several events a talent show, a rodeo, and a water-skiing exhibition.

9. My parents' visit to camp always meant gifts CDs, magazines, candy, and soda.

10. The last thing I remember thinking as we drove away from camp I sure had a good time.

Name: _____ Date: _____

Unit 5: Punctuation 6—Semicolons

Key Ideas

- **A semicolon** is used to separate two independent, related clauses when a coordinate conjunction is not used.

    Example: *Our team was elated; they finally won the regional tournament.*

- **A semicolon** is used to join two independent, related clauses when the second clause begins with an adverb such as *however, therefore, in fact,* or *consequently.*

    Example: *We arrived late; in fact, we missed most of the game.*

Practice

Directions: Add a colon (:) or a semicolon (;) to the sentences below.

1. Suddenly, Sydney noticed the tiger watching him he couldn't move a muscle.

2. He was frozen stiff however, he did let out a squeak for help.

3. Our guide gave him this advice "Don't move a muscle!"

4. Only two solutions presented themselves shoot the tiger, or scare it away.

5. It was a very trying time for Sydney he was frightened to death.

6. A pride of lions came into sight consequently, the tiger moved off on his own.

7. Sydney was greatly relieved however, it took him days to recover from his experience.

8. Our tour guide said "It happens."

9. We were all very quiet however, we looked at Sydney to see his reaction.

10. Finally, he laughed however, I don't think he will ever be the same again.

On Your Own: Check out your most recent library book. Look for examples of colons and semicolons. See if you can determine from the rules above why the writer used either the colon or the semicolon.

91

Unit 5: Punctuation 7—Quotation Marks

Key Ideas

- Use **quotation marks** any time you use someone else's exact words.
  Example: *Maggie said, "I really enjoy my job."*

- If they are not the exact words of the speaker, don't surround them with quotation marks.
  Example: *Maggie said that she really enjoys her job.*

- When writing dialogue, start a new paragraph every time you switch from one speaker to another.
  Example: *"Did you enjoy your visit to the pig farm?" my teacher asked the class when we returned from our field trip.*
  "Oh, yes," we responded enthusiastically, "but it did smell funny."

- **Quotation marks** are used with titles of poems, short musical works, television shows, and articles from magazines and newspapers.
  Example: I enjoy "Laughter Is the Best Medicine" in *Reader's Digest.*
  She titled her poem "An Ode to Spring."

Practice

Directions: Imagine a conversation between yourself and your parent(s). You've been asked to go to Walt Disney World by a friend from school your parent(s) do(es) not know. You have to provide money for your airplane ticket, but your friend's parents will take care of the rest. Write at least four sentences of this conversation on the lines below.

_____

_____

_____

_____

_____

_____

_____

_____

On Your Own: Turn this beginning dialogue into a persuasive essay following the format presented earlier in this book.

Unit 5: Capitalization 1—Confusing Capitals

Key Ideas

- Do not begin a common noun with a **capital letter**, even when it refers to a proper noun just mentioned.

  Example: *I live in the state of Michigan.*

- Titles and rank (and their abbreviations) begin with **capital letters** when they occur with names.

  Example: *General George Feducka, Jr.*

- Ranks or titles that appear alone do <u>not</u> begin with **capital letters**.

  Example: *One of the generals came by to see you.*

- Family relationships, however, when used as names and appearing alone may be **capitalized**.

  Example: *Where is Nana?*   *She is with Mom.*

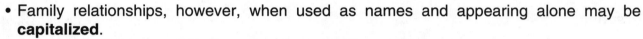

Practice

Directions: Rewrite each sentence, capitalizing where appropriate.

1. Our teacher brought our class a present from general norton when she returned from her visit to the state of washington.

   _____

   _____

2. I won't be at practice, coach, because we are having a birthday party for my mother.

   _____

   _____

3. melissa said to her mother, "thank you for packing such a good lunch yesterday, mom."

   _____

   _____

4. we wanted to go to the museum in the city, but it was closed.

   _____

   _____

5. the museum of modern art has many fine paintings.

   _____

Name: _____ Date: _____

Unit 5: Capitalization 2—Geographical Names

Key Ideas
- **Capitalize** geographical names such as cities, states, countries, continents, bodies of water, geographical features, and geographical areas. Do not capitalize small words like *the*, *and*, and *of*.

    Example: *Rock of Gibralter*
    Empire State Building
    Amazon River

- **Capitalize** nationalities, races, languages, religions, religious terms, and specific school subjects followed by a number.

    Example: *Korean*   *Farsi*
    Algebra II   *Caucasian*

Practice

Directions: Edit the following sentences by using the editor's mark (Ξ) to indicate where capital letters are needed.

1. The state of florida lies between the atlantic ocean and the gulf of mexico.

2. The cities of munich, marseilles, and warsaw are all on the european continent.

3. Does the tropic of cancer run through mexico, argentina, or panama?

4. In israel, a middle-eastern country, hebrew is the official language.

5. In what hemisphere do you find both north america and south america?

6. The suez canal joins the red sea with the mediterranean sea.

7. The people in puerto rico speak both spanish and english.

8. Is new zealand northeast or southeast of australia?

9. Which is the saltiest body of water: the pacific ocean, the dead sea, or the great salt lake?

10. Niagara falls borders both the united states and canada.

Unit 5: Capitalization 3—Special Events

Key Ideas
- **Capitalize** names of holidays and other special events, streets, highways, buildings, bridges, monuments, historical events, periods of time, and documents.

    Example: *American Revolution*   *Sears Building*
    Ambassador Bridge   *Route 66*

- **Capitalize** the names of organizations, businesses, institutions, and agencies.

    Example: *National Football League*   *Youth Soccer League*
    Girl Scouts   *Child and Family Services*

Practice

Directions: Using the editor's mark for capitalization ($\equiv$), correct all words in these sentences that should be capitalized.

1. The state of illinois is called "the land of lincoln."

2. The comet called halley's comet was named for the astronomer edmund halley.

3. If the local currency is the ruble, are you in russia, austria, or romania?

4. The emancipation proclamation freed the slaves in the confederacy in 1863.

5. Franklin d. roosevelt was president of the united states during the great depression.

6. Bill clinton was the president who appointed ruth bader ginsburg to the u.s. supreme court.

7. Which of these names is not a palidrome: otto, bob, mimi, or anna?

8. The artists manet, monet, and renoir were impressionist painters.

9. If you flew from hawaii to japan, you would cross the international date line.

10. The scientist wilhelm roentgen won a nobel prize in 1901 for the x-ray.

On Your Own: Make up a trivia question of your own that contains at least three of the rules for capitalization above. Give it to a friend, and have him or her correct it.

Name: _____ Date: _____

Unit 5: Capitalization and Punctuation Test

Directions: Read each item and look for the punctuation mistake, if there is one. If there isn't, darken the circle beside "No mistakes." Darken the circle that represents the best answer.

1. ○ A. "What American holiday
   ○ B. is the unofficial end of
   ○ C. summer," our teacher asked.

2. ○ A. "Labor Day," Sam shouted
   ○ B. from the back of the room.
   ○ C. No mistakes

3. ○ A. Sam noticed
   ○ B. the teacher watching him
   ○ C. He froze in place.

4. ○ A. "Is that how we answer,"
   ○ B. the teacher asked Sam.
   ○ C. No mistakes

5. ○ A. We were all very quiet
   ○ B. however, we looked at Sam
   ○ C. to see his reaction.

6. ○ A. The first rule of survival
   ○ B. Fall silent when the teacher
   ○ C. is staring at you.

7. ○ A. "I welcome your contribution
   ○ B. anytime, Sam that you raise
   ○ C. your hand," the teacher said.

8. ○ A. Sam smiled another lesson
   ○ B. learned the hard way.
   ○ C. No mistakes

9. ○ A. For his first week in school,
   ○ B. Sam had a good day,
   ○ C. a bad day and a so-so day.

10. ○ A. One thing is certain
    ○ B. Sam learned the lesson
    ○ C. he was supposed to learn.

Directions: Read each sentence. Choose the sentence or group of words that shows the correct punctuation and capitalization. Darken the circle next to the correct choice.

11. ○ A. John F. Kennedy international airport is New York City's largest airport.
    ○ B. John F. Kennedy International airport is New York city's largest airport.
    ○ C. John F. Kennedy International Airport is New York City's largest Airport.
    ○ D. John F. Kennedy International Airport is New York City's largest airport.

12. ○ A. Montana is known as "the big sky state."
    ○ B. Montana is known as The Big Sky State.
    ○ C. Montana is known as "the Big Sky State."
    ○ D. Montana is known as the big sky state.

13. ○ A. Henry Wadsworth Longfellow wrote *The Midnight Ride of Paul Revere*.
    ○ B. Henry wadsworth longfellow wrote The Midnight Ride of Paul Revere.
    ○ C. Henry Wadsworth Longfellow wrote The midnight ride of Paul Revere.
    ○ D. Henry Wadsworth Longfellow wrote "The Midnight Ride of Paul Revere."

Name: _____ Date: _____

Unit 5: Capitalization and Punctuation Test (cont.)

14. ○ A. "I only regret that I have but one life to lose for my country said nathan hale.
    ○ B. I only regret that I have but one life to lose for my country said Nathan Hale.
    ○ C. "I only regret that I have but one life to lose for my country" said Nathan Hale.
    ○ D. "I only regret that I have but one life to lose for my country," said Nathan Hale.

15. ○ A. No, I don't know in which movies Kirk, Spock, and the klingons appeared.
    ○ B. No, I don't know in which movies Kirk, Spock, and the Klingons appeared.
    ○ C. No I don't know in which movies Kirk, Spock, and the Klingons appeared.
    ○ D. No, I don't know in which movies Kirk spock, and the Klingons appeared.

16. ○ A. Order from west to east; Russia, Finland, Iceland
    ○ B. Order from west to East: Russia, Finland, Iceland
    ○ C. Order from west to east, Russia, Finland, Iceland
    ○ D. Order from west to east: Russia, Finland, Iceland

17. ○ A. Which city was not founded by the French: San Antonio, Detroit, or New Orleans?
    ○ B. Which city was not founded by the french? San Antonio, Detroit, or New Orleans?
    ○ C. Which City was not founded by the french, San Antonio, Detroit, or New Orleans?
    ○ D. Which city was not founded by the French; San Antonio, Detroit, or New Orleans?

18. ○ A. Basketball uses these terms, dunk, dribble, foul shot.
    ○ B. Basketball uses these Terms: dunk, dribble, foul shot.
    ○ C. Basketball uses these terms: dunk, dribble, foul shot.
    ○ D. Basketball uses these terms dunk, dribble, foul shot.

19. ○ A. Mary shelley, wife of the poet, wrote Frankenstein.
    ○ B. Mary Shelley wife of the poet wrote *Frankenstein*.
    ○ C. Mary Shelley, wife of the poet, wrote Frankenstein.
    ○ D. Mary Shelley, wife of the poet, wrote *Frankenstein*.

20. ○ A. lake erie and the hudson river were joined by the erie canal.
    ○ B. Lake Erie and The Hudson River were joined by The Erie Canal.
    ○ C. Lake Erie and the Hudson River were joined by the Erie Canal.
    ○ D. Lake Erie and the Hudson river were joined by the Erie canal.

Unit 6: Spelling 1—Remembering the *ie/ei* Rule

Key Ideas

- Conventional **spelling** is an important part of writing because writers want to communicate the correct meaning to their readers.

- Use *i* before *e* except after *c* or when it sounds like "ay" as in *neighbor* and *weigh*.
    Examples: *"ie"*: *belief, field, friend, mischief, niece, patience, piece*
    "c": *ceiling, deceit, deceive, receipt*
    "ay": *eight, sleigh*

- There are some common exceptions that you must memorize.
    Examples: *caffeine, counterfeit, height, neither, weird*
    "c": *conscience, financier, science, species*

Practice

Directions: Choose the correct spelling for each word in parentheses and circle it.

1. My mother (beleived, believed) that my sister and I created the mess.

2. She disobeyed the sign that said (*Yeild, Yield*).

3. The clerk forgot to give Eric a (receipt, reciept) for his purchase.

4. The police tracked the (theif, thief) through the dark by his light-up sneakers.

5. Have you ever visited a (foreign, foriegn) country?

6. Alicia (reveiwed, reviewed) my essay before I revised it.

7. A (freight, frieght) train derailed in the middle of town, causing chaos with the traffic.

8. Jason, Janelle, and I all got to see the (anceint, ancient) mummy skeletons at the museum.

9. Sherry reported a (feiry, fiery) crash at the racetrack last Saturday.

10. Shamus didn't like (either, iether) the book or the movie made from the book.

On Your Own: Collect in your personal dictionary other words that are exceptions to this rule. How many do you think there are?

Name: _____ Date: _____

Unit 6: Spelling 2—Adding Suffixes

Key Ideas
- Conventional **spelling** is an important part of writing because writers want to communicate the correct meaning to their readers.

- When adding most suffixes to a word ending in *y*, change the *y* to *i* if the letter before the *y* is a consonant; keep the *y* if the letter before the *y* is a vowel.
  Examples: *friendly + er = friendlier*   *happy + ly   = happily*
  pay + ment = payment   *annoy + ance = annoyance*

- A few exceptions to this rule are very short words ending in *y*, such as *dryly, wryly, shyly, daily, gaily*.

- If the suffix starts with *i*, the *y* **never** changes to *i*.
  Examples: *apply + ing = applying*   *baby + ish = babyish*

Practice

Directions: Add the suffix to the root word and write the word correctly on the line.

1. apply   +   ed   =   _____

2. merry   +   ment   =   _____

3. sunny   +   er   =   _____

4. heavy   +   est   =   _____

5. dizzy   +   ness   =   _____

6. mercy   +   ful   =   _____

7. comply   +   ing   =   _____

8. skinny   +   est   =   _____

9. boy   +   ish   =   _____

10. cloudy   +   er   =   _____

11. beauty   +   fy   =   _____

On Your Own: Use *university + es* and *simplify + es* in a sentence. Find another pair of words that follow one of the rules above, and ask a friend to use both of them in a sentence.

Unit 6: Spelling 3—Confusing Contractions

Key Ideas

- Conventional **spelling** is an important part of writing because writers want to communicate the correct meaning to their readers.

- The words on the left are **contractions**; the words on the right are not. It's easy to make a spelling error by confusing these words. Be very careful when you use them.

it's (it is)	its (of it)
they're (they are)	their (of them)
	there (at that place)
who's (who is)	whose (of whom)
you're (you are)	your (of you)

Practice

Directions: Circle the correct word to complete each sentence. Be sure to choose the right one!

1. I hope (you're, your) very careful when handling those chemicals.

2. (They're, Their, There) harmful when coming in contact with (you're, your) skin, eyes, nose, etc.

3. If you were to spill some, (you're, your) skin would burn and peel.

4. (It's, Its) very nice of you to help out with the cleanup.

5. (You're, Your) a very good helper, Joanna.

6. Just put those chemicals over (they're, their, there) on the teacher's table, please.

7. (Who's, Whose) idea was it to use the chemicals in the experiment, anyway?

8. Maybe that group hasn't completed (they're, their, there) experiments yet.

9. Does anyone know (who's, whose) in that group of students?

10. (They're, Their, There) negligence could be harmful to (you're, your) classmates.

On Your Own: Write a note to this group, explaining why #10 could be true. Use as many of the confusing contractions as you can. Have a friend correct any misspellings.

Name: _____ Date: _____

Unit 6: Spelling 4—One-Word/Two-Word Pairs

Key Ideas

- Conventional **spelling** is an important part of writing because writers want to communicate the correct meaning to their readers.

- Some words can be written either as one word or two. The spelling depends on the meaning.

  Example: *Maybe Enrico is finished.*
  Enrico may be finished.

all ready (completely prepared)	already (previously)
all together (all in one place)	altogether (thoroughly)
all ways (all methods)	always (at all times)
a lot (a large amount)	allot (distribute, assign)
every day (each day)	everyday (ordinary)
may be (could be)	maybe (perhaps)
some time (an amount of time)	sometime (at some unspecified time)

Practice

Directions: Circle the correct words in each sentence.

1. (All ways, Always) check to see if you have considered (all ways, always) of doing the problem.

2. The teacher will (a lot, allot) paint and (a lot, allot) of paper to each group of students.

3. Jordan (all ready, already) asked us if we were (all ready, already) to go on vacation.

4. (Every day, Everyday) my mother gives me a million (every day, everyday) chores to do around the house.

5. Kiku's family (some times, sometimes) spends (some time, sometime) in Japan with her relatives.

6. It (may be, maybe) that Eleanor's mother will say (may be, maybe) she can go with us.

7. The Schaeffer family gathered four generations (all together, altogether) for their family photo. That's (all together, altogether) too many people!

Name: _____ Date: _____

Unit 6: Spelling 5—Confusing Homonyms

Key Ideas
- Conventional **spelling** is an important part of writing because writers want to communicate the correct meaning to their readers.

- The spelling of **homonyms** (words that sound alike but have different meanings) is often confusing. Spelling usually depends on the meaning.

Examples:
dye (color)	die (perish)
dessert (food)	desert (dry land)
pair (two)	pear (fruit)

Practice

waste	capital	weather	lead	gorilla
waist	capitol	whether	led	guerrilla
rain	threw	which	here	weak
reign	through	witch	hear	week
hole	meat	principle	taut	quiet
whole	meet	principal	taught	quite

Directions: Choose the correct word for each blank from the word bank above. Some words may be used more than once.

Our (1) _____ , Mr. Garcia, announced that our (2) _____ class

would take a trip to our state (3) _____. For the past (4) _____, our

teacher, Mrs. Johnson, has (5) _____ us many things about our state. Since (6)

_____ had been in the (7) _____ forecast, we wondered (8)

_____ or not we would go. "The (9) _____ doesn't matter," said Mrs.

Johnson. "We will (10) _____ in front of the school tomorrow at 7:00 A.M." My friend

Shannon and I were (11) _____ happy to (12) _____ this. We could

hardly wait for tomorrow to get 13) _____!

On Your Own: Look for more of these confusing homonyms and similar words in your reading. Write them in your personal dictionary.

Name: _____ Date: _____

Unit 6: Spelling 6—Similar Spellings

Key Ideas

- Conventional **spelling** is an important part of writing because writers want to communicate the correct meaning to their readers.

- Really confusing words are those that are similar in spelling and pronunciation. Sometimes the words are even similar in meaning!
    Examples: breath (noun)   breathe (verb)
                     chose (past tense)   choose (present tense)

Practice

Directions: Read the following paragraph. Look for commonly confused words. Edit using the editor's mark (⬭) for any words that are misused or misspelled. Write the correct word above the circled word.

"Were just about to eat our desert," Dorothy said. "Would you care to join us?"

"Thanks allot, but no. I've all ready eaten—a for-coarse meal," La Keisha said.

"Oh, just have one small peace of pie, plane, without any topping," Dorothy urged.

"It looks delicious," La Keisha replied, "but to tell the truth I've been worried about my waste. I've been trying to loose weight; my cloths are getting so tight I can hardly breath."

"Are you getting any exercise?" asked Dorothy, "that's probable the best way to loose weight."

"I no," La Keisha answered, "but I can't seam to motivate myself. I keep putting it off."

"Hear's an idea!" Dorothy exclaimed. "Why don't we meat tomorrow morning and go for a run?"

"Alright, what a grate idea!" La Keisha exclaimed.

Name: _____ Date: _____

Unit 6: Spelling Test

Directions: Read each set of phrases. One of the underlined words is spelled incorrectly for the way it is used in the phrase. Find the word that is spelled incorrectly, and darken the circle of your choice.

1. ○ A. a deep <u>whole</u>
   ○ B. a <u>pair</u> of socks
   ○ C. a <u>pail</u> of water
   ○ D. a Halloween <u>witch</u>

2. ○ A. bought new <u>clothes</u>
   ○ B. once a <u>weak</u>
   ○ C. two ripe <u>pears</u>
   ○ D. <u>threw</u> the ball

3. ○ A. <u>four</u> cute puppies
   ○ B. <u>some</u> good books
   ○ C. <u>there</u> own house
   ○ D. nice <u>weather</u>

4. ○ A. <u>here</u> the news
   ○ B. burned some <u>wood</u>
   ○ C. take a <u>break</u>
   ○ D. <u>quiet</u> the baby

5. ○ A. <u>led</u> the parade
   ○ B. <u>mail</u> the package
   ○ C. <u>through</u> the window
   ○ D. put it <u>hear</u>

6. ○ A. <u>which</u> one is it
   ○ B. eat your <u>desert</u>
   ○ C. <u>dye</u> your hair red
   ○ D. what is the <u>weather</u> like

7. ○ A. <u>breathe</u> through your nose
   ○ B. <u>choose</u> carefully
   ○ C. eat the apple <u>whole</u>
   ○ D. <u>new</u> the answer

8. ○ A. <u>whose</u> bike
   ○ B. <u>you're</u> going
   ○ C. <u>its</u> nice of you
   ○ D. at <u>their</u> house

9. ○ A. <u>it's</u> wrong
   ○ B. stand over <u>there</u>
   ○ C. <u>who's</u> talking
   ○ D. <u>you're</u> umbrella

10. ○ A. <u>they're</u> not home
    ○ B. <u>their</u> in the house
    ○ C. go over <u>there</u>
    ○ D. <u>you're</u> right about this

Directions: Look at the four words in each item. Fill in the circle for the one that is _not_ spelled correctly.

11. ○ A. mischief
    ○ B. thief
    ○ C. neighbor
    ○ D. freind

12. ○ A. beleif
    ○ B. eight
    ○ C. science
    ○ D. conscience

13. ○ A. reviewed
    ○ B. yield
    ○ C. either
    ○ D. caffiene

14. ○ A. sleigh
    ○ B. reciept
    ○ C. believe
    ○ D. field

Name: _____ Date: _____

Unit 6: Spelling Test (cont.)

15. ○ A. foreign
     ○ B. neice
     ○ C. neither
     ○ D. freight

16. ○ A. ancient
     ○ B. hieght
     ○ C. weird
     ○ D. fiery

17. ○ A. either
     ○ B. species
     ○ C. pateince
     ○ D. piece

18. ○ A. believed
     ○ B. ceiling
     ○ C. deceit
     ○ D. deisel

19. ○ A. liesure
     ○ B. deceive
     ○ C. counterfeit
     ○ D. neigh

20. ○ A. receive
     ○ B. freight
     ○ C. chief
     ○ D. wieght

Directions: Read each sentence. Darken the circle that represents the correct answer.

21. _____ was an exciting one on our recent trip to Mexico.

     ○ A. Every day
     ○ B. Everyday

22. We chose not to go to Spain because we had been there _____.

     ○ A. all ready
     ○ B. already

23. On our next trip, _____ you could go with us.

     ○ A. may be
     ○ B. maybe

24. We always take _____ of suitcases, cameras, and film with us on our trips.

     ○ A. a lot
     ○ B. allot

25. Wherever we go, we _____ have a good time together.

     ○ A. all ways
     ○ B. always

Name: _____ Date: _____

Unit 7: Usage 1—Simple Subjects and Predicates

Key Ideas
- **A simple subject** is the main word (or words) in the complete subject.

   Example: *The man in the orange vest drives the pavement roller.*
   complete subject: *The man in the orange vest*
   simple subject: *man*

- **A simple predicate** is the main word (or words) in the complete predicate.

   Example: *The pavement roller is flattening the new asphalt on the road.*
   complete predicate: is flattening the new asphalt on the road.
   simple predicate: *is flattening*

Practice

Directions: Underline the simple subject in each sentence. Circle each simple predicate.

1. The owners of the comic book shop smiled.

2. Customers were filling their shop.

3. A small, dark-haired boy had been studying one comic

   for 20 minutes.

4. It was a special comic in the *Batman Dark Knight* series.

5. His brother was buying a *Superman, Man of Steel*, comic book.

6. Their father waited patiently by the door as he thumbed through a *Spiderman* comic.

7. He was supposed to be watching his two-year-old daughter.

8. She was running around and under the display tables.

9. The owners caught the little girl as she ran past the cash register.

10. This little incident was very embarrassing to the boys.

On Your Own: Make a list of five nouns and a separate list of five verbs. Exchange your lists with a partner, and ask him/her to write a paragraph using the nouns and verbs on your lists as simple subjects and simple predicates.

Name: _____ Date: _____

Unit 7: Usage 2—Compound Subjects and Predicates

Key Ideas

- **A compound subject** contains two or more simple subjects, joined by words such as *and* or *or*.

  Example: *My aunt and my uncle are celebrating their anniversary.*
  compound subject: aunt and uncle

- **A compound predicate** contains two or more simple predicates, joined by words such as *and* or *or*.

  Example: *They will have a party and take a trip to celebrate.*
  compound predicate: will have and take

Practice

Directions: Read each sentence. Underline the compound subjects, and circle the compound predicates. Not every sentence will have both.

1. Together, my dog and cat have eight legs.

2. After tonight, Haoli and Yin-mei will never speak to or entertain those people again.

3. Tired and hungry, Charles and Anne left the office and went to the restaurant.

4. Those socks and shoes have been in your room or closet for almost a week.

5. You and I walked and ran all the way home from the park.

6. The mother and father opened their umbrellas and dashed to their car.

7. Books, records, and videotapes filled the shelves and spilled onto the chairs in the room.

8. At the beach, my sister and I ate our picnic, swam in the ocean, read to each other, and walked on the sand.

On Your Own: Write a compound subject on a piece of paper. Ask a partner to write a compound predicate on another slip of paper. Exchange. Add what is missing to the sentence to make a complete sentence. Share the results.

Unit 7: Usage 3—Sentence Fragments

Key Ideas

- **A sentence** is a group of words that expresses a <u>complete</u> thought and has both a subject and a predicate.

> **Example:** *The American crocodile is a large, shy reptile.*

- A **sentence fragment** is an incomplete thought; either the subject or the predicate is missing.

> **Example 1:** *American crocodiles.*

It is a sentence fragment because the predicate is missing.

> **Example 2:** *Live along the coast of Florida.*

It is a sentence fragment because the subject is missing.

> **Example 3:** *American crocodiles live along the coast of Florida.*

It is a sentence because (1) it is a complete thought, and (2) it contains both a subject and a predicate.

Practice

Directions: Read each group of words. If it is a sentence, write "sentence" on the line. If it is a fragment, write "fragment" on the line.

1. The American crocodile is a rare animal. _____

2. It has a long, pointy snout. _____

3. Dark gray-green, scaly skin. _____

4. Adult American crocodiles. _____

5. Crocodiles swim very well. _____

6. Moving themselves through the water by their tails. _____

7. Are an endangered species. _____

8. Crocodiles are meat-eaters. _____

9. They can grow to be up to 15 feet long. _____

10. They have 66 teeth. _____

Name: _____ Date: _____

Unit 7: Usage 3—Sentence Fragments (cont.)

Directions: Add predicates to each of these subject parts to make complete sentences. Use each subject once.

- **Crocodile**   • **I**   • **My assistant**   • **His yellow, scaly belly**

1. _____

2. _____

3. _____

4. _____

Directions: Add subjects to each of these predicate parts to make complete sentences. Use each predicate once.

- **are their only enemies.**   • **have smooth scales on their bodies.**
- **live in warm, quiet waters.**   • **is where they live.**

1. _____

2. _____

3. _____

4. _____

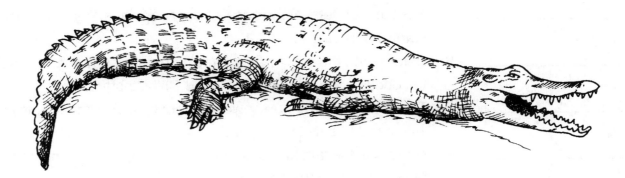

On Your Own: Imagine that you are a famous crocodile hunter. On your own paper, write a five-sentence paragraph to tell about your job. Use the information learned above to help you make up an adventure of your own. Be sure to avoid sentence fragments.

Unit 3: Usage 4—Sentence Run-ons

Key Ideas
- **A sentence** is a group of words that states a <u>complete</u> thought.
  Example: *George Washington wore false teeth.*

- **A sentence** that states <u>two</u> complete thoughts or ideas without the proper punctuation is a **run-on sentence**.
  Example: *George Washington's false teeth made him look funny his cheeks were caved in.*

- **A run-on sentence** can be corrected by separating the <u>two</u> complete thoughts into two sentences.
  Example: *George Washington's false teeth made him look funny. His cheeks were caved in.*

Practice

Directions: Read each sentence carefully. If the sentence contains one complete thought, write "sentence" on the line. If it contains two or more complete thoughts (or ideas) running into each other, write "run-on" on the line.

_____ 1.   The story is that George Washington hired Betsy Ross to make the first flag the flag was called the "Stars and Stripes."

_____ 2.   The story was told by Betsy's grandson, William Colby it was not true.

_____ 3.   He told the story of Betsy Ross during a speech in Philadelphia.

_____ 4.   Colby said he had heard the story from his grandmother and other family members.

_____ 5.   The story of Betsy Ross became very popular everyone liked it and started believing it.

_____ 6.   Before long the story was printed in the newspaper and in school textbooks soon everyone believed Colby's story.

_____ 7.   This story could be true however there is no proof that Betsy Ross was hired to sew the first flag.

_____ 8.   Nobody in the family ever saw her working on the flag no one in the family ever saw the finished flag.

_____ 9.   She did sew flags Betsy made many flags for the United States Navy.

_____ 10.   The story of Betsy Ross may be more fiction than fact.

Name: _____ Date: _____

Unit 7: Usage 5—Verbs That Agree

Key Idea

- Singular subjects take singular **verbs**, and plural subjects take plural **verbs**.

  Example: *Wearing a red hat and yellow socks, Bob was sitting in the box seat section of the ballpark.*

  subject = Bob singular
  verb = was singular

Practice

Directions: Circle the correct verb in each of the sentences below.

1. Andrea (is, are) in the high school marching band.

2. Jessie and Andrea (play, plays) the clarinet, and Emily (play, plays) the flute.

3. Playing a musical instrument (is, are) hard work and (take, takes) a lot of practice.

4. Nathan and Keith (was, were) in the band last year too.

5. Next Thursday at 6:30 P.M. (is, are) the Homecoming Parade.

6. Everyone must (wears, wear) his or her band uniform.

7. Mr. Walton (require, requires) everyone to wear black shoes and socks with his or her uniform.

8. Will your parents (come, comes) to the parade?

9. The high school (is, are) sponsoring a bonfire after the parade (end, ends).

10. The band (practice, practices) every day for the competition next month.

On Your Own: Write a paragraph about an instrument you play or would like to play. Be sure to make your verbs agree in number with your subjects.

Name: _____ Date: _____

Unit 3: Usage 6—More Subject-Verb Agreement

Key Idea
- **A compound subject** with *and* takes a **plural verb**.
  - **Example:**   *Robert, James, and John* all *have* new bikes.

- If **a compound subject** is joined by *or, either ... or,* or *neither ... nor*, make the verb agree with the subject that is closest to it.
  - **Example:**   *Her sisters or <u>Sara is</u> ready to help.*
    Sara or her <u>sisters are</u> ready to help.

- In sentences beginning with *here* or *there*, first find the subject, and then make the verb agree with it.
  - **Example:**   *There <u>goes Sara</u> to help the mothers.*
    Here <u>come Paul and Paula</u>.

Practice

Directions: Circle the verb in parentheses that agrees with the subject in each sentence.

1. Kelly and her friend (take, takes) skating lessons.

2. Neither Kelly nor her friend (like, likes) to practice.

3. Mothers and fathers (watch, watches) every lesson and

    practice.

4. Kelly's mother or her friend's mother (drive, drives) the girls to

    their lessons.

5. Evan or Mason (skate, skates) as Kelly's partner.

6. A coach or an assistant (help, helps) Kelly at each lesson.

7. Either Nicole or Jan (serve, serves) as Kelly's coach.

8. Here (is, are) Kelly's skates.

9. There (go, goes) Kelly's friends gliding across the ice.

10. Kelly's mother and father (enjoy, enjoys) seeing her perform.

On Your Own: Write five sentences that begin with *either ... or* or *neither ... nor,* but leave blanks where the subjects should be. Ask a friend to fill in the blanks with subjects that agree with the verb.

Unit 7: Usage 7—Noun-Pronoun Agreement

Key Ideas
- **A pronoun** must agree with the **noun or other pronoun** to which it refers.
  Example: *I identified that <u>man</u>. <u>He</u> is my neighbor. (<u>He</u> refers to the <u>man</u>.)*

- **An antecedent** is the noun or pronoun that the pronoun replaces.
  Example: *<u>He</u> is my neighbor. (<u>He</u> replaces <u>man</u>.)*

Practice

Directions: Identify the antecedent of the underlined pronoun in each sentence by writing it on the line to the right.

1. Are Lindsey and Ross still at the game, or did <u>they</u> leave? _____

2. When Yasmine and Tiffany left their bikes out in the rain, <u>they</u> rusted. _____

3. Mr. Taylor is ill today; <u>he</u> has the flu. _____

4. Enrique raises pigeons on the roof of the building where <u>he</u> lives. _____

5. Mom washed the curtains, and I hung <u>them</u>. _____

6. Mrs. Jamison has a basketball court in her driveway, and <u>she</u> lets me play on it. _____

7. Soccer is a very popular sport in this town; <u>it</u> is even more popular than football. _____

8. Brooke and Caroline were discussing <u>their</u> vacation plans. _____

9. Marty looks sharp today. <u>He</u> is wearing a red scarf and a dark blue sweater. _____

10. Queenie and Rachel had a very good time at the party, but <u>they</u> had to clean up afterwards. _____

On Your Own: Read a news article from a newspaper or a magazine. Underline the pronouns and circle the antecedents. Exchange with a partner to check.

Name: _____ Date: _____

Unit 7: Usage 8—Adjective-Adverb Mistakes

Key Ideas

- **An adjective** modifies a noun or a pronoun.

    Example: *His ridiculous behavior has angered all his loyal fans.*
    adjective = ridiculous   modifies = behavior
    adjective = loyal   modifies = fans

- **An adverb** tells "how," "how often," "when," or "where." Most adverbs modify verbs.

    Example: *Sam walked slowly down the mountain last night.*
    adverb that tells "how" = slowly
    adverb phrase that tells "where" = down the mountain
    adverb phrase that tells "when" = last night
    all modify the verb walked

- A common mistake writers make is to use **adjectives** when they should use **adverbs**.

    Remember: *Adjectives **do not** modify verbs, adverbs do.*
    Example: *He jogged quickly. (not quick)*
    The team played well. (not good)

Practice

Directions: Read each sentence. Circle the correct word in parentheses to complete each sentence.

1. Ida likes (good, well) food.

2. Her mother, however, doesn't cook very (good, well).

3. She doesn't take the time to measure everything (careful, carefully).

4. Nor does she keep a (careful, carefully) eye on the food while it cooks.

5. One problem is that she (quick, quickly) mixes all the ingredients

    together and then (quick, quickly) stirs, mixes, pours, and boils.

6. She doesn't understand about bringing soup to a (slow, slowly) boil.

7. Instead she (slow, slowly) gathers the ingredients and then boils the

    soup as (rapid, rapidly) as she can.

8. Her bread is the exception; she bakes (good, well) bread with (great,

    greatly) flavor.

9. She bakes (wonderful, wonderfully) without following a recipe, but her cooking is not

    (eager, eagerly) anticipated.

10. Consequently, Ida is (happy, happily) when the family orders out for Chinese food.

Name: _____ Date: _____

Unit 7: Usage Test

Directions: Read each item. Darken the circle that represents the <u>best</u> answer.

1. Which one of the following is <u>not</u> correct?
   - ○ A. Dogs and cats is important to people.
   - ○ B. Dogs and cats are important to people.

2. Which one of the following is <u>not</u> correct?
   - ○ A. Often a cat and its owner become good friends.
   - ○ B. Often a cat and its owner becomes good friends.

3. Which one of the following is <u>not</u> correct?
   - ○ A. In many cases, a dog works hard.
   - ○ B. In many cases, a dog work hard.

4. Which of the following sentences contains a *run-on* sentence?
   - ○ A. I love ice cream it's refreshing.
   - ○ B. I love ice cream because it is so refreshing.
   - ○ C. Ice cream is so refreshing, which is why I love it.

5. Which of the following sentences contains a *run-on* sentence?
   - ○ A. When Kitty ran out the door, she fell into a hole in the backyard.
   - ○ B. Kitty ran out the door she fell into a hole in the backyard.
   - ○ C. Kitty fell into a hole in the backyard when she ran out the door.

6. Which of the following sentences contains a sentence *fragment?*
   - ○ A. The people in this ancient building.
   - ○ B. They locked the doors before leaving.

7. Which of these sentences contains a sentence *fragment?*
   - ○ A. When did you reach the beach?
   - ○ B. When it rained, naturally.
   - ○ C. Neither

8. Which of these sentences is correct?
   - ○ A. The village have a fair today.
   - ○ B. The village has a fair today.

9. Which of these sentences is correct?
   - ○ A. Ashley and Kim share a dorm room.
   - ○ B. Ashley and Kim shares a dorm room.

10. Which of these sentences is correct?
    - ○ A. Jessica, together with Andrea, want to shop at the mall.
    - ○ B. Jessica, together with Andrea, wants to shop at the mall.

Name: _____ Date: _____

Unit 7: Usage Test (cont.)

11. Which of these sentences is correct?
    ○ A. Many fewer money was made at the car wash than expected.
    ○ B. Much less money was made at the car wash than expected.

Directions: In the following questions, identify the underlined part of each sentence.

12. My best friend <u>collects soda cans.</u>
    ○ A. Simple subject
    ○ B. Simple predicate
    ○ C. Complete subject
    ○ D. Complete predicate

13. <u>Her large collection</u> contains over 800 different cans.
    ○ A. Simple subject
    ○ B. Simple predicate
    ○ C. Complete subject
    ○ D. Complete predicate

14. Aluminum <u>cans</u> cover every surface of her bedroom: shelves, desk, table tops, etc.
    ○ A. Simple subject
    ○ B. Simple predicate
    ○ C. Complete subject
    ○ D. Complete predicate

15. Someone <u>purchased</u> a can from Japan for her.
    ○ A. Simple subject
    ○ B. Simple predicate
    ○ C. Complete subject
    ○ D. Complete predicate

16. <u>Buses and trains</u> bring tourists to Chicago and St. Louis every day.
    ○ A. Simple subject
    ○ B. Simple predicate
    ○ C. Compound subject
    ○ D. Compound predicate

17. Buses and trains <u>bring tourists to Chicago and St. Louis and take them home every day</u>.
    ○ A. Simple subject
    ○ B. Simple predicate
    ○ C. Complete subject
    ○ D. Complete predicate

116

Name: _____ Date: _____

Unit 7: Usage Test (cont.)

Directions: Choose the correct verb to make the sentence correct.

18. Tammy and her brother _____ swimming lessons.

    ○ A. take   ○ B. takes

19. Two lifeguards _____ every class.

    ○ A. watch   ○ B. watches

20. Neither Barbara nor her classmates _____ soccer.

    ○ A. play   ○ B. plays

21. Rather, they _____ individual sports more.

    ○ A. enjoy   ○ B. enjoys

Directions: Choose the correct adjective or adverb to make the sentence correct.

22. The band played _____.

    ○ A. loud   ○ B. loudly

23. Taniesha was a _____ eater.

    ○ A. slow   ○ B. slowly

24. She also talked _____.

    ○ A. slow   ○ B. slowly

25. The teacher said Randy had _____ handwriting.

    ○ A. bad   ○ B. badly

26. Now I see how _____ he actually writes.

    ○ A. bad   ○ B. badly

Directions: Choose the correct pronoun to replace the underlined word.

27. Let's send a birthday card to <u>Jon and Jeff</u>.

    ○ A. they   ○ B. her
    ○ C. him   ○ D. them

28. <u>Tatiana and I</u> went to the circus last Wednesday.

    ○ A. She   ○ B. Us
    ○ C. We   ○ D. They

29. Please read your report to <u>Mariel and me</u>.

    ○ A. him   ○ B. we
    ○ C. them   ○ D. us

30. Tell <u>Colin</u> that his father is here.

    ○ A. he   ○ B. his
    ○ C. us   ○ D. him

Name: _____ Date: _____

Section III: Teacher Rubric for Evaluating Student Writing

Topic: _____

Type of Writing: *Expository*   *Persuasive*   *Narrative*

Directions: Circle the number that best describes the quality of the writing.

Features	Not yet	Emerging	Developing	Competent	Strong
Ideas/Content: Is the content focused, original, and interesting?	1	2	3	4	5
Organization: Is the organization clear and helpful to the reader?	1	2	3	4	5
Voice: Would you like to read this piece aloud to someone else?	1	2	3	4	5
Word Choice: Do the words and phrases create vivid pictures in your mind?	1	2	3	4	5
Fluency: Can you feel the sentences flow together as you read it aloud?	1	2	3	4	5
Conventions: Would the writer have to do a lot of editing before sharing this piece?	1	2	3	4	5

Comments: _____

_____

_____

Name: _____ Date: _____

Section III: Student Rubric for Evaluating Peer Writing

Name of Writer: _____

Topic: _____

Type of Writing: *Expository*   *Persuasive*   *Narrative*

Directions: Circle the number that best describes the quality of the writing.

Features	Not yet	Emerging	Developing	Competent	Strong
Ideas/Content: Is the content focused, original, and interesting?	1	2	3	4	5
Organization: Is the organization clear and helpful to the reader?	1	2	3	4	5
Voice: Would you like to read this piece aloud to someone else?	1	2	3	4	5
Word Choice: Do the words and phrases create vivid pictures in your mind?	1	2	3	4	5
Fluency: Can you feel the sentences flow together as you read it aloud?	1	2	3	4	5
Conventions: Would the writer have to do a lot of editing before sharing this piece?	1	2	3	4	5

Comments: _____

_____

_____

Name: _____ Date: _____

Section III: Student Rubric for Evaluating Writing

Topic: _____

Type of Writing: *Expository*   *Persuasive*   *Narrative*

Directions: Check those statements that apply to your piece of writing.

_____   I have a clear and interesting topic that I care about.

_____   My writing is based on my own experience or my own investigation into the topic.

_____   I can sum up my main point in one sentence: _____

           _____

_____   I have a strong beginning that "grabs" my reader's attention.

_____   I have included all important events in the order of their happening.

_____   My writing is easy to follow; each point leads to the next point.

_____   I *show* things happening rather than *telling* about them.

_____   My writing has energy, enthusiasm, and confidence and sounds like me.

_____   My language is appropriate to my topic and audience.

_____   My story reads well out loud.

_____   My writing reaches out to "grab" my reader's attention and holds it right up to the end.

_____   I have a strong ending that leaves my reader satisfied.

_____   There are no significant errors in my paper.

_____   I revised and edited this paper carefully.

Comments: _____

_____

_____

_____

120

Answer Keys

Unit 1: Writing a Personal Narrative (p. 5–6)
1. She linked everyone to her favorite memory.
2. Sounds, smells, sights
3. Yes. Use of first person: I, me, my
4. Yes, the author is excited because it's carnival time again, and she describes the sights, sounds, and smells.
5. Yes, it's a true story told by the person who experienced it.

Unit 1: Writing E-mail (p. 8–9)
Answers may vary slightly.
From: Nick
To: Robin
Date: April 11, 2001
Subject: Accident Check-up

Dear Robin,
I'm just checking that you are O.K. after our accident this morning. Are you still mad at me? It was partly your fault, too, you know. If you hadn't been riding so fast, I would have been able to stop sooner. We <u>both</u> flew over the handlebars, remember!

Anyway, cheer up; gravel cuts never leave scars. Well, I have to run. See you later!

Unit 1: Writing Skills Test (p. 12–14)
1. A
2. C
3. B
4. B, D
5. D
6. A
7. C
8. D
9. B
10. D
11. Teacher check using Ideas criteria.

Unit 2: Writing an Outline (p. 28)
I. Childhood
  A. Born December 2, 1981
  B. Born in Kentwood, Louisiana
  C. Member of the Mickey Mouse Club
II. Family
  A. Parents, Jamie and Lynne Spears
  B. Brother, Bryan, 21
  C. Sister, Jamie Lynn, 8
III. Education
  A. Sophomore in high school
  B. Travels with a tutor
IV. Favorites
  A. Enjoys romance novels
  B. Justin Timberlake
  C. Collects dolls
  D. Solo performing

Unit 2: Writing an Outline (p. 29)
I. Geography
  A. Between Austria and Switzerland
  B. Cold, snowy climate
  C. Central Europe
II. People
  A. Catholic, Protestant
  B. Ethnic groups: Turkish, Italian
  C. German, Alemannic dialect
  D. Population 32,207
III. Government
  A. Voting age: 20 years of age
  B. Hereditary constitutional monarchy
  C. Principality of Liechtenstein
  D. Capital city: Vaduz
IV. Major Cities
  A. Malbun
  B. Ruggell
  C. Balzers
  D. Schaan

Unit 2: Writing Skills Test (p. 32–34)
1. A
2. D
3. C
4. C
5. B
6. A
7. D
8. C
9. B
10. D
11. True
12. True
13. True
14. True
15. D
16. A
17. Teacher check using Organization criteria.

Unit 3: Writing Skills Test (p. 48–50)
1. B
2. C
3. D
4. C
5. D
6. D
7. A
8. D
9. C
10. B
11. A
12. B
13. C
14. D
15. B
16. Teacher check using Voice criteria.

Unit 4: Story Plot 1 (p. 70)
1. Person against person
2. Person against person or person against nature
3. Person against nature
4. Person against self

Unit 4: Writing Skills Test (p. 79–82)
1. A
2. D
3. A
4. C
5. D
6. C

7. A   8. D
9. C   10. B
11. A   12. C
13. D   14. C
15. D   16. B
17. A   18. D
19. C   20. A
21. Teacher check using Word Choice and Fluency criteria.

Unit 5: End Punctuation (p. 86)

1. . or !   2. ?
3. .   4. . or !
5. ?   6. . or !
7. . or !   8. .
9. .   10. ?

Unit 5: Commas (p. 87)

1. When you go out in the snow, wear your coat, mittens, and hat.
2. Preston, did you hear what I said?
3. This child, I swear, would go out in this frigid weather without a coat, if I let him.
4. Margaret, did you notice that last night it rained, snowed, and thundered?
5. Wow! What odd weather we are having, don't you think?
6. What is going on with the weather, I wonder?
7. In this month alone, we have had hot weather, cold weather, rainy weather, and sunny weather.
8. Randall, of course, enjoyed the weather variety.
9. How does he stand all the changes, Marie?
10. Preston, wear your boots!   or
   Preston, wear your boots.

Unit 5: More Commas (p. 88)

1. To win, she worked very hard.
2. Under a tree in the hammock, my father slept.
3. Kamal is a tall, handsome young man.
4. Santa delivered the toys, and Mrs. Santa made the cookies.
5. When I returned from camp, my room was no longer the same.
6. Today was a hot, sunny day.
7. Penny brought the blanket, and Dylan brought the flashlight.
8. To go on the field trip, Thomas had to sell 14 boxes of cookies.
9. We played well, and we were happy.
10. Edward is a loud, boisterous player.

Unit 5: Colons (p. 90)

1. The first chore assigned to me at camp: laundry.
2. One thing is certain: The new person at camp always has to do the worst job.

3. Given the terrible weather of the last few days, I was relieved by what was coming: nice, sunny, dry days.
4. I strode up to the dozens of washing machines in the laundry and quoted John Paul Jones: "I have not yet begun to fight."
5. Finally, I got to participate in the activities I came for: games, swimming, and riding.
6. There were children of many different nationalities at camp this year: American, Asian, English, German, Spanish, and French.
7. There is one lesson I learned at camp: Everyone is basically the same.
8. During the last week, we participated in several events: a talent show, a rodeo, and a water-skiing exhibition.
9. My parents' visit to camp always meant gifts: CDs, magazines, candy, and soda.
10. The last thing I remember thinking as we drove away from camp: I sure had a good time.

Unit 5: Semicolons (p. 91)

1. Suddenly, Sydney noticed the tiger watching him; he couldn't move a muscle.
2. He was frozen stiff; however, he did let out a squeak for help.
3. Our guide gave him this advice: "Don't move a muscle!"
4. Only two solutions presented themselves: shoot the tiger, or scare it away.
5. It was a very trying time for Sydney; he was frightened to death.
6. A pride of lions came into sight; consequently, the tiger moved off on his own.
7. Sydney was greatly relieved; however, it took him days to recover from his experience.
8. Our tour guide said: "It happens."
9. We were all very quiet; however, we looked at Sydney to see his reaction.
10. Finally, he laughed; however, I don't think he will ever be the same again.

Unit 5: Confusing Capitals (p. 93)

1. Our teacher brought our class a present from General Norton when she returned from her visit to the state of Washington.
2. I won't be at practice, Coach, because we are having a birthday party for my mother.
3. Melissa said to her mother, "Thank you for packing such a good lunch yesterday, Mom."
4. We wanted to go to the museum in the city, but it was closed.
5. The Museum of Modern Art has many fine paintings.

Unit 5: Geographical Names (p. 94)

1. The state of Florida lies between the Atlantic Ocean and the Gulf of Mexico.
2. The cities of Munich, Marseilles, and Warsaw are all on the European continent.
3. Does the Tropic of Cancer run through Mexico, Argentina, or Panama?
4. In Israel, a middle-eastern country, Hebrew is the official language.
5. In what hemisphere do you find both North America and South America?
6. The Suez Canal joins the Red Sea with the Mediterranean Sea.
7. The people in Puerto Rico speak both Spanish and English.
8. Is New Zealand northeast or southeast of Australia?
9. Which is the saltiest body of water: the Pacific Ocean, the Dead Sea, or the Great Salt Lake?
10. Niagara Falls borders both the United States and Canada.

Unit 5: Special Events (p. 95)

1. The state of Illinois is called "the Land of Lincoln."
2. The comet called Halley's Comet was named for the astronomer Edmund Halley.
3. If the local currency is the ruble, are you in Russia, Austria, or Romania?
4. The Emancipation Proclamation freed the slaves in the Confederacy in 1863.
5. Franklin D. Roosevelt was President of the United States during the Great Depression.
6. Bill Clinton was the president who appointed Ruth Bader Ginsburg to the U.S. Supreme Court.
7. Which of these names is not a palidrome: Otto, Bob, Mimi, or Anna?
8. The artists Manet, Monet, and Renoir were Impressionist painters.
9. If you flew from Hawaii to Japan, you would cross the International Date Line.
10. The scientist Wilhelm Roentgen won a Nobel prize in 1901 for the x-ray.

Unit 5: Capitalization and Punctuation Test (p. 96–97)

1. C	2. C
3. B	4. A
5. A	6. A
7. B	8. A
9. C	10. A
11. D	12. C
13. D	14. D
15. B	16. D
17. A	18. C
19. D	20. C

Unit 6: Remembering the *ie/ei* Rule (p. 98)

1. believed	2. *Yield*
3. receipt	4. thief
5. foreign	6. reviewed
7. freight	8. ancient
9. fiery	10. either

Unit 6: Adding Suffixes (p. 99)

1. applied	2. merriment
3. sunnier	4. heaviest
5 dizziness	6. merciful
7. complying	8. skinniest
9. boyish	10. cloudier
11. beautify	

Unit 6: Confusing Contractions (p. 100)

1. you're	2. They're, your
3. your	4. It's
5. You're	6. there
7. Whose	8. their
9. who's	10. Their, your

Unit 6: One-Word/Two-Word Pairs (p. 101)

1. Always, all ways   2. allot, a lot
3. already, all ready   4. Every day, everyday
5. sometimes, some time
6. may be, maybe
7. all together, altogether

Unit 6: Confusing Homonyms (p. 102)

1. principal	2. whole
3. capital	4. week
5. taught	6. rain
7. weather	8. whether
9. weather	10. meet
11. quite	12. hear
13. here	

Unit 6: Similar Spellings (p. 103)

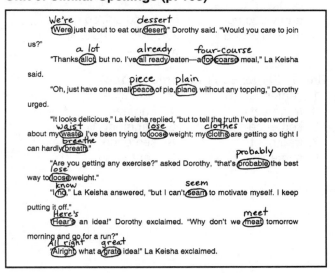

Unit 6: Spelling Test (p. 104–105)

1. A	2. B
3. C	4. A
5. D	6. B
7. D	8. C
9. D	10. B
11. D	12. A
13. D	14. B
15. B	16. B
17. C	18. D
19. A	20. D
21. A	22. B
23. B	24. A
25. B	

Unit 7: Simple Subjects and Predicates (p. 106)

Simple Subject	Simple Predicate
1. owners	smiled
2. Customers	were filling
3. boy	had been studying
4. It	was
5. brother	was buying
6. father	waited
he	thumbed
7. He	was supposed to be watching
8. She	was running
9. owners	caught
she	ran
10. incident	was

Unit 7: Compound Subjects and Predicates (p. 107)

Compound Subjects	Compound Predicates
1. dog and cat	have
2. Haoli and Yin-mei	will speak or entertain
3. Charles and Anne	left and went
4. socks and shoes	have been
5. You and I	walked and ran
6. mother and father	opened and dashed
7. Books, records, and videotapes	filled and spilled
8. my sister and I	ate, swam, read, and walked

Unit 7: Sentence Fragments (p. 108)

1. sentence	2. sentence
3. fragment	4. fragment
5. sentence	6. fragment
7. fragment	8. sentence
9. sentence	10. sentence

Unit 7: Run-on Sentences (p. 110)

1. run-on	2. run-on
3. sentence	4. sentence
5. run-on	6. run-on
7. run-on	8. run-on
9. run-on	10. sentence

Unit 7: Verbs That Agree (p. 111)

1. is	2. play, plays
3. is, takes	4. were
5. is	6. wear
7. requires	8. come
9. is, ends	10. practices

Unit 7: More Subject-Verb Agreement (p. 112)

1. take	2. likes
3. watch	4. drives
5. skates	6. helps
7. serves	8. are
9. go	10. enjoy

Unit 7: Noun-Pronoun Agreement (p. 113)

1. Lindsey and Ross	2. bikes
3. Mr. Taylor	4. Enrique
5. curtains	6. Mrs. Jamison
7. Soccer	8. Brooke and Caroline
9. Marty	10. Queenie and Rachel

Unit 7: Adjective-Adverb Mistakes (p. 114)

1. good	2. well
3. carefully	4. careful
5. quickly, quickly	6. slow
7. slowly, rapidly	8. good, great
9. wonderfully, eagerly	10. happy

Unit 7: Usage Test (p. 115–117)

1. A	2. B
3. B	4. A
5. B	6. A
7. B	8. B
9. A	10. B
11. B	12. D
13. C	14. A
15. B	16. C
17. D	18. A
19. A	20. A
21. A	22. B
23. A	24. B
25. A	26. B
27. D	28. C
29. D	30. D